From Ordinary to Extraordinary

Book 1
Preparation and Commitment

(Workbook Included)

ATIYA

ATIYA'S LIGHT
PUBLISHING

ARIZONA   CHICAGO   LONDON

First Published 2010 by Atiya's Light Publishing
ISBN 978-0-615-42253-4

This Second Edition Published by Atiya's Light Publishing, 2014

Copyright © 2010, 2014 by Atiya K.M.

All rights reserved. No part of this publication may be reproduced, distributed, or transmitted in any form or by any means, or stored in a database or retrieval system, without the prior written permission of the publisher.

Atiya's Light Publishing
818-658-5533
www.atiyaslight.com
info@atiyaslight.com

Front Cover Photo by Donald Barge
Author Photo by Chas Richardson

Library of Congress Control Number: 2014902772
ISBN: 978-0-9916444-0-7

Printed in the United States of America

*For my children,
Kharisma (Ashley), Khadijah and Khalil*

*Be bound
in love and favor,
yet be loosened and freed
from your past.
No matter which direction you face,
love still conquers all.*

Acknowledgments

Here, I graciously and humbly acknowledge THE ONE who opens the magnificent gateway and allows the creation of all that is. I acknowledge ALL IN ALL that is good, positive, loving, kind, compassionate, and peaceful. I acknowledge the truth and the light and all of those who are seekers of the truth and the light.

I acknowledge the genuine and joyful smile, which is the "kiss" of the heart. No matter how many times I fall, I acknowledge that this is a journey and I will become more seasoned with time.

Table of Contents

Introduction 1

1 17

Knowing and Embracing Who You Are 17

    Chapter One Monologue: Maggie, Who Are You Really? 31

    Life's Lesson: 39

    Words of Wisdom: 40

    WORKBOOK PART 1 41

2 61

Assessing and Being Who You Are 61

    Chapter Two Monologue: Find the Power Within .. 70

    Life's Lesson: 76

    Words of Wisdom: 76

    WORKBOOK PART 2 77

3 85

Learning to Love the You That You Discover 85

    Chapter Three Monologue: Arise and Come Forth! 99

Life's Lesson: 103

Words of Wisdom:... 103

WORKBOOK PART 3 104

4 115

Exercising Your Power to Be 115

Chapter Four Monologue: The Woman From Tekoa
.... 124

Life's Lesson: 127

Words of Wisdom:... 129

WORKBOOK PART 4 130

5 139

Keeping Your Eyes on the Prize........................ 139

Chapter Five Monologue: Do You Trust Me?......... 151

Life's Lesson: 156

Words of Wisdom:... 158

WORKBOOK PART 5 159

Conclusion 165

From Ordinary to Extraordinary

Book 1: Preparation & Commitment

Introduction

As human beings, we experience many changes in our lives. Throughout the course of our journey, we discover various aspects of our being daily. In the quiet moments of our mind, we sometimes find ourselves searching for the purpose of life and the answer to that infamous question - "Who am I?"

While some of us may not openly admit it, we often question the Creator and ourselves about whom we really are, how we came to be, why at this moment in time have we been born and for what purpose. Yet, that voice within, answers. Although it may sometimes appear faint, better still, it's there within each of us, and has the answer to everything we could ever want to know about who we are. The key is within.

Do you realize that you have the ability to achieve greatness and reach your highest potential? Do you know that you have been born into the world with an innate capacity to become master of your endeavors?

Do you understand that you have been shaped into perfection and given the wonderful opportunity to perfect even what many refer to as perfection? Well, you do, you can and you will.

For those of you who doubt perfection exists, this is what is meant. The Originator, Supreme Source, Creator, or whatever name you choose to recognize THE ONE as, has fashioned you complete in your physical makeup. Biologically, you were equipped with the tools necessary to live a purposeful life on a physical plane. With infinite wisdom, THE ONE created you as a multi-dimensional being, and left it up to you to cultivate and refine the gifts and talents bestowed upon you when you were just a consideration.

Perfection is said to be the highest and most excellent standard. However, the determination of perfection is often measured by someone else's opinion of what perfection looks like and whether or not it has been achieved. To perfect perfection is to move beyond the limitations of others.

The creation of you is of the highest standard and without error or mistake. At conception, a portion of

Introduction

THE ONE was deposited in you. As you came forth from your mother's womb, THE ONE whispered into your soul the very purpose for which you were created. You were equipped with gifts that serves as evidence that THE ONE not only exists and lives within you, but also that you were, from the beginning, destined to be an extraordinary being.

There is a birthright to be claimed upon the successful nurturing of the gifts that you have within. Your gifts are not only the doorway for luxury, money, good homes and friendships in all walks of life, they also serve as your doorway to experiencing the many other dimensions of your life, particularly that spiritual aspect which connects you to THE ONE.

You are capable of thinking far beyond even the highest degree of excellence. There is no limit to what you are able to do. You are boundless beyond expression, and the more you tap into the depths of your being and mine out those precious jewels from within, the more you realize who you are and why you are. The little voice is there within, guiding you every step of the way.

The first step on the ladder of success is the knowledge of self. The second is the courage to be yourself. THE ONE is not only the force and power who stands between you and that first step, THE ONE is the very foundation, framework, and platform on which the steps even exist.

So now, it's fair to propose the following questions. Why and how does stagnation occur? Why does it appear extremely difficult to live and walk in the shoes of our life's purpose? Why in such a magnificent universe to which we were born to master, does it appear to be so far out of reach to simply take our gifts and secure benefit for ourselves and families?

Why are countless beings unable to take their place in this majestic universe—as the stars that light the heavens and the earth? Why do so many, fall short of exuding the confidence of that of the sun, as she shines brightly over both the just and unjust?

The sun consistently does what she was created to do and does it so naturally and effortlessly. She shines, and she allows no one or nothing to interfere with her shine. Can you imagine the great amount of effort it would take for the sun to hide her light?

As the most glorious creation of THE ONE, we were born to rule and master the sun. Yet, the effort it would take the sun to hide her light, is the same amount of effort we act like it would take us to let our light shine. Many people have become motionless beings allowing others to move them according to whatever whim or fancy they have at the moment. Why is it that some are unable to stay in motion in the direction of their purpose, or find it so easy to alter their motion, as others come along playing musical chairs with their life?

Scores of people go through life "letting it happen" to them. They appear to aimlessly exist, inattentively occupy space, and lack the luster to experience the real joy and meaning of life. Perhaps, they do so, as a result of not believing they can achieve greatness beyond their most creative imagination. What do you think? Many people have yet to discover the extraordinarily beautiful being that lies within. Each one of us holds the key to becoming wonderful, magnificent and new.

The point is this: you hold the power to your evolution. I'll say it again. Y-O-U, hold the power to your own evolution. In reality, you are that fascinating person you have periodically envisioned in your mind's eye. While you may not fully comprehend it at this moment, it's a matter of you deciding to BE, and then becoming who you really are, naturally. You get the honor and privilege to decide. What an awesome opportunity!

Joy, peace, contentment, and real meaning of life, comes only through a communion with the Self. The "Ultimate Self" is that unseen force masked within every human being, including you. It is the quiet, still voice you hear from within. It's the spirit of consciousness, which does not lie. It is honest with you and prompts you to be accountable and responsible with your life—the most valuable gift that you have been given.

The Ultimate Self is THE ONE who defines you. Think about this for a moment. The Ultimate Self is the greatest, the most high, the supreme. The Ultimate Self is unsurpassable. Your self in submission to the Ultimate Self is a dance that demonstrates perfect precision of time.

When others witness this exquisite display of rhythm, one cannot help but to move to the flow of the beat. It's just natural to groove to the tone, which aligns all. The world and environment in which you live are tools to measure your effectiveness as to how well you are presenting the Ultimate Self; how well you are living your truth. When you go contrary to the internal messages of truth, you impact the harmony and congruency of things within and without.

Not playing life in tune with the Ultimate Self upsets the balance of your being and wreaks havoc on your system. You have been created in truth, and the Ultimate Self only recognizes and cooperates with truth. So, whenever any human being goes in contrary to the reality in which they were created, the Ultimate Self recognizes the contradiction and wages war against falsehood in order to restore balance.

Those who live in fear and reject truth, perpetuate the inequity by being silly asking questions to which, they already know the answer. The Ultimate Self revealed what you wanted to know, in truth naturally.

As soon as the thought entered into your mind, or you quietly wondered about something, intuitively you immediately knew the answer.

You may not have trusted it, but the answer was present. You were created in the nature of truth. While you may choose to go against the grain of truth, the fact of the matter is that truth always remains consistently true. In the spirit of truth, the Ultimate Self is the truest of truths.

There is no need to wallow in self-pity or feel that you are not understood. Sure you may question your adequacy and wonder when your turn will come. It has always been your turn. So, there's no sense in continuing to secretly desire to be your self, and express the beauty within. Just do it!

Start from this moment accepting who you are and being yourself. Cast out fear and be you freely. Others will soon catch on to the reality that you are truly extraordinary and a wonderful glimpse of the Ultimate Self. They will soon see you as a magnificent creation in the universe.

It's not necessary to blame others for your own fear to BE, nor is it necessary to ask the Ultimate Self,

"Who am I?" That question has been answered many times over; perhaps you have not listened or believed the answer that you've received. Know that you are and declare that you are! Live! You're free to say in the presence of your being – "I AM, that I AM."

When you say, "I am that I am," you are actually stating, "The person who stands before you is a manifestation and product of what is in my mind. I exist and shall remain by virtue whatever image I form in my own mind." In other words, you are what you think you are; therefore, think better of your self, who is a reflection of the Ultimate Self.

It's amazing how some people search for solutions to problems that really don't exist, and for answers to questions, which they intuitively know the answer. In their quest for truth, they often deny the Ultimate Self, and attempt to make falsehood fit as truth. When in truth, they know the truth about themselves already. They fumble around hoping others will accept their truth, yet refuse to present their truth to be accepted.

In conscious awareness, it is easily understood that two solid things cannot occupy the same space at the same time. One must give way to the other. Further, some things just don't fit in nor was created to fit. On the other hand, some things were made to fit and when those things come together, very little effort is needed.

Without having to ask anyone else, every human being on the face of the earth knows naturally when something does not fit and when something does. Nevertheless, many try to force a thing that doesn't fit, and then get disappointed afterwards. Why would a person do such a thing? Could it be the desire to gain access or raise one's status? Is it really access or status a person desires or is it something else?

Have you perchance thought that maybe, just maybe they simply want acceptance? Not recognizing the Ultimate Self or facing the truth of one's self is a perversion. It's an entrapment in a continuous and aimless parody. The self is an idea in the mind of the Ultimate Self. You exist and remain by what is in the mind of the Ultimate Self. Yet, if you are confined to the mental bondage of inferior thoughts, you will become inferior in your presentation, and misrepresent the truth of who you are, and negate your self, rendering yourself ineffective.

If you are one of those people who have been doing this, it is time for you to willfully be truthful and start being and doing you. Consider this a wakeup call - a conscious call. This is a summons to you to discontinue sending mixed messages to your subconscious, which is unable to differentiate between truth and falsehood. She is submissive regardless as to whether you are lying or being truthful. However, consciously, even she wages war against a lie. She knows who you really are.

Real acceptance only comes from the Ultimate Self. At the end of the day, truth will only fit, and falsehood cannot occupy the space where truth is and when truth is. The answer to the question lies deep within. If you let it, the control dramas of others will dictate and convince you that you don't know the answer, when you really do.

You don't have to be cloudy or filled with doubt in your own abilities. A world built on an approval system does not have to color what you know inside to be true. The Ultimate Self never lies. You have always known the answer. If you have not been living in truth, then you have simply just been afraid to trust the Ultimate Self. So this time when you ask yourself "Who am I?" accept the answer, then, BE. Start now living through the truth of the Ultimate Self.

My friend and fellow traveler, this is an exciting time. I graciously invite you to join me on this extraordinary journey into self-discovery, acceptance, and mastery. My aim is to inspire you to find the power within yourself to connect with the Ultimate Self and cooperate in your own transformation. "I AM that I AM."

It's simply me, speaking from the heart and creative force of my being, as I am experiencing communion with the Ultimate Self. By sharing with you the essence of the Ultimate Self within me, hopefully it will arouse you to connect with the Ultimate Self within you and inspire you as it has me.

Each chapter of this book is divided into four parts. The first part is the Communion or the sharing of thoughts and emotions. The second part is the Monologue or the story that brings character to the thoughts as they happen. The third part deals with the

Life Lessons learned from the meditations after reflecting on the thoughts shared. Finally, the fourth part provides Words of Wisdom, insights or intuitive understanding of the thoughts. So now, please join me on this journey From Ordinary to Extraordinary? Are you ready? Let us begin together.

ಐಔ

Re-create yourself every step of the way and never
stop believing in the magical moments that come
from finding your inner-child.

1

Knowing and Embracing Who You Are

The journey to greatness begins with knowing and accepting who you really are. To know you is to experience you. Life gives you those experiences, whether positive or negative. To find joy and contentment, it's necessary to go within the essence of your being. To find acceptance, you must learn the many aspects of yourself and embrace the diversity within, seeking to completely understand the fascinating being of who you are.

Only when you have learned to accept every aspect of yourself, including your so-called flaws, will you begin to see a glimpse of your destiny. It is your absolute truth. Succumbing to fear, worthlessness, envy and an overwhelming need to please others is the act of holding back. It interferes with your ability to get to know yourself and the Ultimate Self. It is possible to find the "flawless" beauty within. However, it takes you looking into that proverbial mirror, which may sometimes be very difficult.

Once you finally take a look, developing a high regard for what you see, may prove to be an even greater challenge. It takes courage to look into the depths of your soul and warmly invite your being to a quickening of the spirit. Every human being has a creative side. However, many allow their light to be put out by those around them. They allow their gifts to be suppressed and their person to be oppressed. If they don't get that nod of approval from others, they tend to lose their self-confidence and sight of what they wanted or should have been doing.

There is no need to feel unacceptable or spend a lot of energy worrying about what others think about you. It's counterproductive to your own greatness to continuously attempt to improve yourself by emulating those you believe to be more acceptable. Learning from a person with an exemplary character is one thing, but to deny yourself to your own detriment is not to appreciate the life that you have been given.

How you view yourself and others is a matter of perspective and dependent upon the frame of mind you are in at the moment. Are you in a healthy state of mind? What constitutes an exemplary character? What factors determines or qualifies a character being better over another?

Hug yourself. Love yourself. Allow your Ultimate Self to guide you to greatness. You've had the power within from the time you were born into the world. To unleash it, you must accept yourself without condition. No one else compares to you. You are unique and magnificent. Open your loving arms and welcome a truly fascinating person – YOU.

It's understandable that it may be a struggle to embrace who you are. Often times this happens when a person inadvertently allow others to make them feel less than or undeserving of all that their heart desires. Your greatness is not measured by the value others place on you. It is only determined by the value you place on yourself. You determine your own self-worth. A person establishes their value by what they do with their life. The same applies to you. Your life is a precious gem that must be cared for and polished in order to see its brilliance.

People come in and out of our lives for many reasons. Each encounter is to teach a lesson and build the spirit. Some may devalue you because of the experiences you've had in your life, whatever those experiences might have been. People simply make excuses as to why they do not interact with others. These excuses almost always boil down to a status issue. Nothing and no one has the ability to devalue us without our permission.

We give others the go-ahead to interfere with our self-worth when we do not embrace ourselves. How can we expect others to appreciate us, when we do not show appreciation and gratitude for self? It takes boldness to show up in truths clothing and stand with your head up regardless as to where you are in your life or where you have been.

Courage is a characteristic that helps us to face difficulty. It is an attribute inherent in all of us, but so often masked. Courage is a candid photograph of the heart. It captures the very essence of our being and helps us to embrace ourselves unconditionally. Be courageous!

It's so amazing and sometimes unbelievable at the lengths people go to hide their insecurities. When envy and jealously shows its ugly head, it targets those who have a false sense of pride or strength and it seeks itself in us. Envy will attempt to define you, and keep you in a cycle of self-negation; by keeping you focused on what it has made you to believe is not right about you.

Envy keeps you coveting what you think and feel to be right about others. It is a beast that feeds off of the energy it steals. Yet, in all of its seductive persuasion, envy is no match for truth, courage and self-determination.

When one fails to embrace who they are, it is usually because they are ashamed of how they have been presenting themselves. Many feel humiliated and blame themselves for simply letting things happen to them and accepting whatever comes their way. Are you one of those people?

You may not necessarily be the cause of all of your circumstances. So don't allow your condition to dictate who you are and shape how you feel about yourself. Be assured that you are far above your station in life. Where you are at the moment is only an indication of how you feel about yourself and the impact of past decisions.

If you are not satisfied with where you are at this moment in time, then make another choice. Determine to change your condition. You have the power to send your mind where you want to be, and then call your body to the party. The great thing is, we all have the right to change our minds. More importantly, we all have the right to self-determination.

As we grow and develop, it's very likely that we will consistently make better and more suitable choices. When we embrace ourselves, we give others permission to do the same. I dare you, go ahead. Be true to yourself. Even when others think you are not worthy of all the wonderful things you deserve, embrace yourself and know that there is no one more deserving to be included and embraced than you.

This is not selfishness or self-absorption. It is about appreciating yourself and finding value in the gift that you are to the world. There are people who in order to make themselves look better, seem to always find something wrong with the next person. Don't fall for those psychic attacks.

Commit yourself to learning your Ultimate Self, being uninhibited in discovering everything about yourself. This is what facilitates understanding of the Ultimate Self, and brings you to an acceptance of whom you really are and what you were born to do.

When you seek out yourself, the field is so vast, the creation of you is infinite, and THE ONE'S love for you is undying and through it, never ceases to create. Nonetheless, the seeking of yourself must start with the reflection that you see when you look into the mirror. Live freely and in your truth.

We are all constantly changing and evolving. So, to stop looking within the self, one ceases to exist. To experience eternal life, is to continue in this circle of evolution of the knowledge of the Ultimate Self. The more you search the depth of truth within, the closer you come to the Eternal Source – THE ONE – The Ultimate Self.

As you continue the discovery process, you realize more and more that on this evolutionary journey, there really is only ONE and we are all extraordinary expressions of THE ONE. What causes discord and disharmony are two little seeds called fear and doubt. Yet, where did these seeds come from?

Fear stagnates, and tosses one out of the circle of evolution. Doubt hinders you from overcoming fear. The same is true when one has an overwhelming need to please other than the Ultimate Self. If you allow your motion to be dictated by others outside of the Ultimate Self, the tendency is confusion within self.

Chaos occurs when there is inconsistency in the internal and external messages. Truth is always confirmed. When you listen to the Ultimate Self which is within, you will always recognize truth. Veracity always sets well with you, even if the message calls for self-correction. Confusion is a sign that you are not listening to the Ultimate Self. There is no reason to be confused. You are great. Everything about you is beautiful, because everything about you has potential.

Release yourself from guilt, insecurity and the inferiority complex you may have allowed to linger.

Exonerate yourself from uselessness, worthlessness and despair. These are all secondary thought processes you have been conditioned to believe. Travel within the depths of your being and see the wisdom and beauty that lies within. It has only remained dormant because fear has captured and enslaved you. Doubt has kept you there. You're free now. So, live freely.

Discover the truth about yourself. Realize that uselessness and worthlessness is a figment of someone else's imagination. Allow no one's superiority complex to effect how you feel about yourself. Celebrate your magnificence. Be grateful for your extraordinary beauty. Allow your thoughts to be original, creative and joyful.

Beware of second-hand thoughts, which can depress you and suppress your creativity, if you let them. Sharing creative and original thoughts increases the flow of your creativity. Further, it enables others who are recipients of your sharing to be more creative as well.

You are free to choose life and live it joyously at peace being who THE ONE is inspiring you to be.

Relinquish the bondage of the past to fully accept the power of The Supreme in your transformation. Resolve to evolve!

In life we all do things that we may not be proud of or regret. However, consider each day another blessed day that we have been given to do better. Make yourself available for your future. Live in the now, but make yourself available for your future.

If you're tied to your past and fixed to the way things "used to be", then you are not free to grow and move on to a greater reality. Growth requires change. If you are holding on to your past too tightly, it will become difficult to make the necessary revisions, alterations, modifications, and improvements your life may need. Change is necessary when one seeks to move from being ordinary to extraordinary.

Change requires reconsideration and deep reflection. Your future depends on a willingness to make changes and move from your present level of thought. This is not to say, forget your past or ignore the present. This is encouragement to settle the things of your past, which need settling, and put them in their proper place.

If you are unwilling to let some things go, then you will not be able to see where you are at the moment in proper perspective. Thus, you become limited in moving forward. No matter how much you try, your past is just that – your past. If you do not learn the lessons of your past, you will most likely repeat them.

Where you are at the moment is a consequence of past decisions. Your present state and how you respond now determines the outlook of your future. If you are stuck in a time warp, then your present condition won't serve as the bridge it is designed to serve to your future. You'll simply stay in a cycle of repeating the same things over and over, while making no real growth or upward mobility. This cycle prohibits you from growing and evolving.

When we are bonded to the things of our past, it becomes even more necessary to send strong intentions out into the universe for a release. When we are unable to let go of past issues, we experience blockages which keep us from flowing in the universal flow of things. Sincere meditation and acknowledgment of THE ONE - Supreme Source - the Ultimate Self is a higher state of awareness. The act of acknowledging THE ONE calls the essence of self to attention and sends a vibration within activating the alignment process - aligning your entire being back into ONENESS. Being in total alignment helps things to move and flow the way they were intended to flow and move.

The more you travel within the essence of yourself, the more you become aware of your thoughts. Meditation and acknowledgment is the act of traveling within and the beginning of putting forth thoughts into motion. Don't panic; just dispel the thoughts that you do not choose, and nurture the thoughts that you do choose.

Let no one bound you to the mistakes of your past. Forgiveness destroys negative thought processes and love reinforces positive thought processes. Include yourself to experience inner peace and joy. You are free to give yourself the love you strive so hard to give others. Accept good choices, not compulsion. You are free. Be Free.

Allow yourself not to be burdened by trivialities. It only divides your energy. Focus on the constant

Knowing and Embracing Who You Are 29

travel through space that allows you to continuously experience the profound beauty and love of THE ONE. Seek to understand the true meaning of the senses, for they are the tools to experience. Deprive envy and jealousy of thought and energy. They kill the spirit. Instead feed hope and encouragement to self. They give birth to the spirit, while love sustains it.

Learning to love yourself is truly learning to love THE ONE. Learning to love THE ONE allows you to love others. LOVE IS ONENESS. Treat yourself to the best of everything, not accepting what is left over. In addition to treating others how you want to be treated, be sure to treat yourself how you want others to treat you.

Be who you choose to be, not what others try to make you. Ask yourself each day who you are, and then BE. Create your own reality and invite those in that you choose. Control your own atmosphere and call to you the best of things. Mediocrity has no place in your life. Make this journey of life always seeking the best and most excellent. Be the best example you can be. Be true to yourself. Get to know that hidden side of yourself. You know the side that no one sees, or you think they don't see. That is the side to which I am referring. The Ultimate Self sees all.

The hidden qualities you possess, represents your true self. It is that particular part that will teach you. Strive to unite the many aspects of yourself. This enables perfect harmony and exquisite balance within the self. There's no reason to doubt or cling to the idea that others make you who you are. When you are able to rely completely on the power within, confusion will dissipate.

Learn to appreciate yourself. We so often live for others when we would be more fulfilled if we lived for the Ultimate Self. However, living for THE ONE does not mean living up to the ideas that others have mandated to be the "Will of God." Living for the Ultimate Self is allowing your body, mind and spirit to unite into oneness and cultivate the essence of self, which is contained within the Ultimate Self and one with THE ONE. The essence of self is the Ultimate Self. Rely on the greatness within, rather than depend on the uncertainty that is outside of self. THE ONE is all-encompassing – ALL IN ALL.

When we put expectations on others that in reality they may not live up to, we set ourselves up for disappointment. Accept others for who they are and they will be encouraged to accept you for who you are. Remember, we do not have the power to change others, but through our example of excellence and joyous living, we have the creative power to inspire.

Unity and peace is experienced through having a thorough knowledge of self. Knowing yourself is the beginning of peaceful living and the pathway to unity. Take the time to get to know you. Explore you. Eliminate the self-imposed guilt complex that you are being selfish just because you have the courage to BE. Create time to get to know you, then embrace - the you, - that you discover.

Chapter One Monologue: Maggie, Who Are You Really?

Well, well, well. It's nice to see so many fine men and oh of course, women. I'm Magdalene; but please, by all means, call me Maggie. Most of you think that you know who I am. I see you every time I walk into the room. The same faces, the same stares. You men glance and smile, wishing that I would oblige your invitation. You high-society women just turn up your noses, daring your man to give me a second look. Some say I'm very peculiar. Others think I'm cheap. Those who have had the pleasure of my company know that I don't come cheap. Huh? Don't worry, I won't tell your dirty little secrets. Tonight, I'm telling my own.

So you ask me, "Maggie, who are you really?" Well, I thought you'd never ask. I would be most honored to say. I hope you don't mind, but I'm about to get real personal with you. I shan't lie to you, nor will I pretend anymore. I'm so tired of acting, like I don't have a heart. I'm no cheap thrill that goes from man to man and bed to bed. Sure, I've done some things I'm not proud of, yet what difference does it make. I've done what most of you have thought about. So, in truth who is better? I've probably been the most honest one in here, and I've been lying. I have been masquerading around here like I don't have a heart and like I'm happy where I am in my life.

Today, Maggie's gonna give it to you frankly, and if you're too straight-laced or stuffy to hear my truth, then you might as well leave now… because I'm gonna give it to you straight; I mean, real straight. I can't say it won't get hot. I don't have time to be particular about how I say what needs to be said. I don't have time to be "socially or politically correct" and all. I just want to say my peace. After that, you can go on with business as usual. You wanted to know, and believe me, I've been dying to tell you - literally. So here it is.

You know, I didn't grow up with the mother, the father, the charming white house with the picket fence. I watched my father for months as he was dying, trying to take care of me. He was a good man, but stricken with disease. He told me, "Maggie, you're a beautiful girl, use your charm." He said, "Men will take care of you, if you let them." So that's exactly what I did. I let men take care of me. That ain't much different from most of you in here. The only difference is, I came at a higher price.

You see, I love parties. I love pretty things, and yes, I love sex. Don't tell me about love, because my daddy taught me to sell my love as a girl. After that cancer that was growing inside of 'em, killed him, I told myself that no decent man would want someone like me. So, I had to take care of myself and this was the only way I knew how.

I was robbed of me. I've been searching my whole life trying to find myself. I didn't have a mama. She died having me. What I wanna have a child for? Don't you know the pain a girl feels when she has no mother? I vowed for every tear cried, there would be one more dollar added to the cost of my time.

Father knew what men liked. He taught me well, didn't he? He could no longer provide for me. However, he taught me how to provide for myself. He had a dignified send off. You know why? It is because I paid the price. After he died, I sold everything he had, and left that miserable existence and came here to start a new life. I left that old life behind me, so I thought. Huhm!

When I came to town, I arrived as a lady. All gentlemen callers wanted to know who to call. They soon learned that I wasn't the kind of girl a respectable man could bring home to meet mother dear. Sure,

Knowing and Embracing Who You Are 35

I played the role well, for a while. But, no amount of acting could hide the tendencies, you see. I had to survive, and I was very good at it.

Taking care of men was not foreign to me, so why shouldn't I? They took care of me. That's a fair exchange, don't you think? It didn't matter if they were married or not. I made no demands of them and I bore them no children. They were warm and full. They could come and go as they pleased. They kept me smiling, smelling good, and looking good.

I gave them adventure. They gave me a little peace of mind. Women, you know exactly what I mean. Maybe you don't. Well, let me tell you, I've traveled this land, accompanying many on their business trips. Shopping while they were at their meetings was a favorite pastime. Buying pretty little frillies, sweet perfume and something tantalizing for their tongues, kept the fantasy alive.

When they return to their quarters, I obliged them of whatever fancy they could conjure up in their heads. It is not all bad. I have seen the world. I wear the things women like you only fantasize about wearing. I perform for them things you dare not do, for fear of being viewed as you now view me.

I attend your elitist social gatherings standing arm and arm with the wealthiest of men. I hold my head up with the appearance of no shame, while flaunting my false sense of freedom at women functions. I put on facades to placate my lack of self-worth. At the end of the day, I return to my small demure cottage on the lake, regretting how I made an utter fool of myself again.

I pray for the strength to finally be delivered of this continuous mirage. Somehow, I keep tying myself in knots. Are there any regrets? Sure, there are always things that you wished were not so. Being tossed to and fro, from one social setting to another is not the ideal life.

I try to control myself. However, what I really regret is trying to be acceptable to you - the status quo! Somehow I kept yielding myself to the highest bidder. I don't want to do this anymore! I won't do this anymore! The truth is I feel hopeless. How can I get out of this cat and mouse game?

Yes, I know the truth of my heart. I can even recognize the truth with each of you. Never underestimate how keen my perception really is. I've played many of you. I've quieted my voice within, to keep you happy and satisfied. I am not interested in doing that anymore. My truth conflicts with you. Most of you have self-righteous indignation. I wanted to be accepted. As a result, I allowed my actions to be ruled by others. NO MORE! NO MORE!

I'm admitting today, that I regret, how loosely I've conducted myself. I'm remorseful of the number of men who have shared my bed, none of whom have been my husband. My heart is heavy. How can I ever forgive myself? How will I ever forgive you? How can I forgive my father? I resent him for what he did to me. I resent you for being offended by my presence. I'm ashamed. It's hard to look at myself in the mirror.

As pitiful as it is, when I look at many of you women in here today, staring at me with such disgust, I see me. It appalls me to even look at many of you? That's why I refuse to look you in your eyes. You too have lied. You have been no more truthful than I have.

Well, I want to be myself—whoever that might be. Maybe I'm a painter, because of all of the beautiful portraits I have painted. Maybe I'm a graceful dancer, for I have danced quietly to find the calm in my world.

Maybe I'm a poet, because I have written my hearts song throughout the years. Whoever I find myself to be, I shall be truthfully. One thing I know to be true about myself is that I love the eternal spirit with all of my heart.

I'm totally enamored by the Godly man, that man of truth. I want to devote my life, my true self to that one who understands me most. He is somewhere out their searching for me. I know he is looking.

No longer shall I be shamed. I will find a way to recapture the innocence I once knew as a young girl. I will never again hide behind a false sense of self. I shall be content at being myself. I will enjoy every moment of the discovery process. So, who am I really? I am Magdalene Gabriella Elita. I will spend the rest of my days discovering who she really is.

Life's Lesson:

Don't let your downfall be your own hand upside your head. In other words, stop beating yourself up. Accept yourself as you are, but strive to become better. We all come with baggage. If you don't like the one's you are carrying, get some new luggage. If you believe your load is too heavy, work to lighten it.

There will always be someone who questions your value or who wonders in their mind if you're good enough. So what! Everyone has their own set of issues. Regardless as to what we measure ourselves by, or who feels we don't measure up, it really doesn't matter. What matters is how securely you are plugged into the Supreme Source; how well you are flowing in the universal flow of oneness.

Accept and BE who you are. Y-O-U is the answer to who am I. It's plain and simple. Remove the titles, the education, and whatever else colors the real you. At the end of the day, you are still you—special and unique. There is no one else in the world like you.

The titles you hold don't add one atom's weight of "special." They only cause others to view you in relationship to your title.

You are so much, more than what others see on the surface. In the big picture, titles don't matter. What does matter, however, is your connection with the Ultimate Self and how well you are manifesting that reality. Are you living joyously, peacefully and are you creating? Truth is Boss! So find truth within yourself.

Words of Wisdom:

- ❖ Never stop looking in the mirror; that way, you will be sure to find the blemish first!

- ❖ Create your own world or someone will make one for you and prescribe an agenda for you as well.

- ❖ If you don't accept yourself, you will always be seeking acceptance from others.

- ❖ Find out who you are, then just be YOU!

WORKBOOK PART 1

Section I – All About You

Directions for Completing the Questionnaire: The Self-Evaluation Questionnaire is designed to help you evaluate and examine specific areas in your life which have an impact on the quality of your life; identify areas in your life that you may want to change to experience a more balanced lifestyle; to bring to your conscious awareness hidden issues and factors that may have a bearing on your effectiveness, happiness and success; help in the clarification of goals; and finally, to lay a foundation which helps you to prepare for a transformation and new beginning.

This is for you. Only share the information with others if you choose to do so. It is very important that you answer honestly and be totally transparent with your thoughts and your feelings. Answer all questions thoroughly, directly, leaving none blank.

1. Who are you?

2. What are four (4) things that are very important to you in life?

3. Have you developed a mission for your life? If so, what is it? If not, why not?

4. Do you believe that change is necessary in your life? If so, why? If not, why not?

5. Not withstanding the above question, what areas of your life do you believe or feel can benefit from change?

6. Why do you feel change is necessary in those areas of your life?

7. What do you hope to accomplish from the changes you make in your life?

8. Have you outlined any personal goals for your life? If so, what are they? If not, why not?

9. Have you outlined any professional goals for your life? If so, what are they? If not, why not?

10. Have you outlined any spiritual goals for your life? If so, what are they? If not, why not?

11. What are the four (4) most important things you would like to accomplish within the next year?

12. What are nine (9) things that you would like to accomplish in your lifetime?

Knowing and Embracing Who You Are

13. What are the three (3) greatest challenges for you at this time?

14. What is the number one stressor in your life?

15. What course of action do you take to minimize the number one stressor in your life?

16. How does your effort in minimizing the stressors in your life help?

Observations & Thoughts

Journal your observations and thoughts from Section I. Start a journal notebook specifically for this book. This will be your first journal entry.

Section II – Rating The Various Areas of Your Life

On a scale of 1 to 10 (1 - being very dissatisfied and 10 - being very satisfied) please rate the following areas of your life as they appear at the moment.

a). Marriage
b). Family
c). Friends
d). Profession
e). Romance
f). Finances
g). Health
h). Time
i). Purpose
j). Skills

k). Parenting
l). Environment
m). Spirituality
n). Recreation
o). Education
p). Social Life
q). Your Life
r). Self Worth
s). Goal Achievement
t). Integrity Level
u). Personal Growth
v). Commitment Level
w). Personal Value
x). Significant Other

Observations & Thoughts

Journal your observations and thoughts from Section II. This will be your second journal entry. Continue on as in previous entry.

Section III – Focal Points

Please answer the questions as completely and thoroughly as possible. Be completely honest. This is about you and not the expectations other have for you. Use a separate sheet of paper.

1. What motivates you?

2. How do you tend to sabotage yourself?

3. How do you best learn?

4. How do you manage and relieve stress?

5. How do you relax?

6. What do you like to do for fun and enjoyment?

7. What do you normally do to take care of yourself?

8. What do you believe are your areas of weakness?

9. What are your strong points?

10. What have you given up on in life?

11. When were you the most happy in your life?

12. Why was the above time the most happiest for you?

13. When were you the unhappiest in your life?

14. Why was the above time the unhappiest time for you?

15. If you could have anything in the world, what would it be?

16. What do you want your life to be about?

17. What is the one thing that you have always wanted to experience, but haven't?

18. If money, family, or other factors weren't an issue, what would you be doing in your life right now?

19. What is the one thing you would do even if you weren't paid for doing it?

20. What is one characteristic about yourself that makes you unique from every other human being?

21. What makes you feel unworthy and undervalued as a human being?

22. What makes you feel appreciated and valued as a person?

23. What would it take for you to accomplish to make you feel self-worth?

Observations & Thoughts

Journal your observations and thoughts from Section III. This will be your third journal entry. Complete a journal entry for this section, follow course as above for all journal entries.

Section IV – Spot Check

Mark true or false for each group of questions. At the end of each group total the number of true statements. At the end determine which areas need specific focus. This will give you a spot check of how satisfied you are with your current condition, and allow you to look at the areas in which you are not happy with in order to make changes. This spot check can be done on a monthly basis to gauge the effectiveness of the changes you are making in your life. Be completely honest. Usually your first answer is the more accurate of how you feel.

WORK
(True or False)

- ❖ My work stimulates me.

- ❖ I am proud of my profession and the work that I do.

- ❖ I feel appreciated at work.

- ❖ I respect the people I work with.

- ❖ I know the direction my career is going.

- ❖ I promptly respond to emails and other messages (24-48 hrs).

- ❖ I'm timely with paperwork so that it does not pile up.

- ❖ I complete my work within a reasonable amount of time.

❖ I managed time fairly well.

❖ I delegate work appropriately and without feelings of guilt.

How many/10 (True Statements)

**FINANCES
(True or False)**

❖ I am satisfied with my income.

❖ I utilize a budget and stick with it.

❖ I pay my bills on time.

❖ I am aware of my debts and when they will be paid in full.

❖ I have a financial plan in place.

❖ I reward myself without feeling guilty.

❖ I use credit cards that I may hold responsibly and wisely.

❖ I have a will.

❖ My wallet/purse/briefcase/book bag is uncluttered.

❖ My taxes are current.

How many/10 (True Statements)

HOME ENVIRONMENT
(True or False)

- ❖ I am happy with my home.

- ❖ My home is generally clean/tidy.

- ❖ I surround myself with things I appreciate and love.

- ❖ My home is clutter-free.

- ❖ I recycle at home.

- ❖ My personal files are organized and in order.

- ❖ My bed supports me having a good and restful sleep.

- ❖ I usually make my bed on a daily basis.

- ❖ I have photos of loved ones on display.

- ❖ I am happy with my mode of transportation.

How many/10 (True Statements)

HEALTH & BODY
(True or False)

- ❖ I am happy with my current weight.
- ❖ I do some form of exercise a minimum of three times per week.
- ❖ I have a balanced diet including lots of fresh food.
- ❖ I do not smoke or drink alcohol excessively.
- ❖ I drink at least 2-liters of water each day.
- ❖ My medical and dental check-ups are up-to-date.
- ❖ I am happy with the amount of sleep I get.
- ❖ I have appropriate and adequate clothes for work and play.
- ❖ I am not concerned with stress levels.
- ❖ I feel well over all.

How many/10 (True Statements)

RELATIONSHIPS
(True or False)

- ❖ I am happy with the level of intimacy in my life.

- ❖ My mate and I have mutual respect and are relationally equal.

- ❖ I get along with my work colleagues.

- ❖ I make amends easily with those whom I have had conflict.

- ❖ I trust the significant people in my life.

- ❖ I know my neighbors and am on speaking terms with them.

- ❖ I consider myself to be a good friend.

- ❖ I see people who are important to me on a regular basis.

- ❖ My friends and family know how much I care about them.

- ❖ I am satisfied with my social life.

How many/10 (True Statements)

PERSONAL
(True or False)

- ❖ I like myself.

- ❖ I've had a celebration of my life in the last two years.

- ❖ I have a life outside of work.
- ❖ I have the confidence to do what I want in life.
- ❖ I have adequate holidays/holy days each year.
- ❖ I am honest and do not exaggerate.
- ❖ I am comfortable saying no when I need to.
- ❖ People know they can count on me to keep my word.
- ❖ I can recall the last time I really laughed.
- ❖ I have a form of creative expression.

How many/10 (True Statements)

SPIRITUAL
(True or False)

- ❖ I feel connected to a Higher Source.
- ❖ I attend a spiritual house at least once per month.
- ❖ I read materials to help with spiritual development regularly.

- ❖ I engage in spiritual conversations with others.

- ❖ I have at least one friend who shares my belief system.

- ❖ I journal on a regular basis.

- ❖ I believe there is a purpose to my life.

- ❖ I am a charitable person.

- ❖ I pray/meditate daily.

- ❖ I am confident with myself as a person.

How many/10 (True Statements)

SELF-DEVELOPMENT
(True or False)

- ❖ I know what I am good at doing.

- ❖ I read a variety of books, materials, and information.

- ❖ I keep up-to-date with current events.

- ❖ I create lists and keep notes of important dates.

- ❖ It's necessary to take the time to learn new things.

- ❖ I am a critical thinker.

- ❖ Appearance and how I present myself is important to me.

- ❖ I am open and honest with people.

- ❖ I attend workshops, seminars, trainings at least twice per year.

- ❖ I set short-term and long-term goals.

How many/10 (True Statements)

SOCIAL
(True or False)

- ❖ Having a social life is important to me.

- ❖ There's mutual respect among my circle of friends/associates.

- ❖ I go out to have fun at least once per week.

- ❖ I make it a point to meet new people.

- ❖ When I'm out for fun, I do not talk about work.

- ❖ I am comfortable with myself when among other people.

- ❖ I don't feel pressured to engage in various activities when out with others.

- ❖ I enjoy being around other people.

- ❖ People enjoy being around me.

- ❖ I am happy with my social life.

How many/10 (True Statements)

PURPOSE
(True or False)

- ❖ I know what I was born to do.

- ❖ I can identify my strengths.

- ❖ I have a life mission.

- ❖ I do internal reflections regularly.

- ❖ People tend to ask for my help with specific things.

- ❖ I am happy with what I am doing in my life.

- ❖ I know at least one talent/gift that I have.

- ❖ I am passionate about at least one thing in my life.

- ❖ It is important that I leave a legacy.

- ❖ I know how I can make a difference in the world.

How many/10 (True Statements)

SCORING SECTION IV

Step One: Add up all of the true statements in each category, and record them on the line after each perspective category.

Step Two: Place the name of each categories on the lines provided in order of lowest number of true statements to highest.

Step Three: Add up all of your true statements and record it on the line next to 100% (e.g. 75/100%) and also next to the strongest area percentage.

Step Four: Add up all of your false statements and record it next to the weakest area percentage.

Step Five: Record your (5) strongest/highest and (5) weakest/lowest categories on the lines provided.

This will give you a spot check of how satisfied you are with your current condition, and allow you to look at the areas in which you are not happy with in order to make changes. This spot check can be done on a monthly basis to gauge the effectiveness of the changes you are making in your life. It's all a part of the journey! So embrace it!

CATEGORIES & SCORES
(Example: Relationships = 9; Finances = 7)

TOTAL SCORE FOR THIS SPOT CHECK

What Percentage/100% (True Statements)

Total Number in Strongest Area % (True Statements)
Total Number in Weakest Area % (False Statements)

WEAKEST AREAS
(List the names and scores in the weakest areas)

STRONGEST AREAS
(List the names and scores in the strongest areas)

For the Month/Year of:

Observations & Thoughts

Journal your observations and thoughts from Section IV. Continue as previously.

೫൦ೃ

Love is a personal thing, and the projection of it starts with what you see in the mirror.

2

Assessing and Being Who You Are

The journey to greatness is a personal one. We must not evaluate ourselves in reference to others. Instead, analyze self for the purpose of determining where you are at the moment, and how far you are from where you would like to be. Looking deep within to find and cultivate the gifts that may have remained dormant for a long time, will prove to be one of the greatest rewards received along the way. You may discover that the gifts you uncover will bring you the greatest satisfaction and fulfillment in life.

It's a miracle to mine out and cultivate the hidden treasures buried far beneath the surface. It is a blessing to bring forward your gift for all to experience. When we learn everything about ourselves, and embrace who we are unconditionally, we are better able to appreciate and accept what we find. This way of assessing takes courage. However, it helps us to bring to light and develop the heart to become exactly who we have been created to be.

Of all the many, wonderful, magnificent and exciting things to be, being yourself is the most beautiful. It takes knowledge of self and courage to be who we are intended to be. What's even more fascinating is that change continuously takes place. Therefore, view change as renewal and growth. Let go of fear and doubt. Accept the freedom to be you. Don't worry if what you find is undesirable to your own spirit. Simply purge it from your existence and make a more pleasing choice.

Many of us tend to reject things about ourselves when someone else determines it to be undesirable. However, what do you really think of the matter? Is your decision to reject a thing based on your belief that it is not acceptable or do you eliminate it for the sake of appeasing someone else? You are not obligated to continue the practice of validating self by others, living up to other's expectations, and being a pawn in someone else's world. Instead, let the Ultimate Self validate you, live up to your own expectations and create your own realm of possibilities by plugging into the Ultimate Self—the source of all power.

It's unnecessary to waste time daydreaming of grandeur. It is possible for you to accomplish the grand things you envision and to claim happiness too. So why continue teasing yourself by working to the point of success, but never open its door?

Remember, the first step on the ladder of success is the knowledge of self. The second is the courage to be yourself. THE ONE is not only the force and power that stands between you and the first step, THE ONE is the foundation, the framework and the platform on which the steps even exists. Acquiring the knowledge of self, accepting and being who you are is a great achievement. Loving yourself is profound!

Open up to experience life. Live life and experience the many beautiful realms of realities. Accept the power you have and rejoice in the spirit of good things and truth. Don't you dare give your power away to lies and deceit! Increase it through love.

Did you know that rejecting yourself is fallacious reasoning? This misconception occurs due to the lack of information about one's self and the relationship with the Ultimate Self. It's important to look internally and examine yourself very closely and truthfully. However, when doing so, think originally and choose freely from your own thoughts and not the opinions and judgments that someone else has injected into your atmosphere. Understand that someone else's views may very well be in contrary to the Ultimate Self. When you have a strong relationship with the Ultimate Self, a gap is closed and it is easier to eliminate confusion.

All things are not for all people. What's for me may not necessarily be for you and visa versa. Stop succumbing to mental and creative bondage, and control dramas. Assess yourself based on truth. We all know undoubtedly deep within the essence of our beings, where we are in our lives, and where we really desire to be.

Don't compromise your own self-worth and dignity. Expose the truth of self by reaching for the truth of the Ultimate Self and BE who you choose to become. Claim your destiny. Stand on your right to self-determination.

Be a courageous spirit. Let the Ultimate Self guide you and increase your will to continue moving forward on this journey of extraordinary living. Build your nerves to stand on truth and stay in the light.

When one maintains integrity, they open themselves up to what truly belongs to them. Integrity isn't only about being of sound character, it is also about living in your own truth and according to what is in your heart. Yes, this can be challenging. However, the key is to be constant in your resolve. Understand this one important point though: Living in your truth requires responsibility and balance. While consistency is important, avoid confusing consistency with stagnation.

Be you today, and be you tomorrow, but understand that you are constantly and consistently changing. What was true about you yesterday is not true today. What is true today may not be true tomorrow.

Therefore, when conducting an assessment of yourself, be sure to accept the ever-evolving self. Learn to flow in a continuous state of transformation. Remember change is renewal.

Think about this for a moment. Electricity and energy can only move by being conducted through a conduit or vessel. Otherwise, it stays suspended in space. In this case, the material is present in space but lacks motion. Electricity and energy conducted through a vessel eventually wears the vessel out. Therefore, change must take place in order for the electricity and energy to continue to travel. The same is true with us. We must continue to grow and transform, in order to continue to be.

An assessment is performed several times over the course of one's life. It's not something that is done only once in a lifetime. We will find ourselves conducting an assessment at every interval of change.

Whenever thoughts of change are produced, assessment is necessary. It's the transition stage of change. Assessments give you the necessary information needed to move forward. It helps you to

Assessing and Being Who You Are

outline what areas need to be addressed at that moment in time.

Assessing your assets is taking an inventory of yourself at that point and time. It's the process of analyzing one's self, and done to determine how far you are from where you want to be, as mentioned earlier in this chapter. Your assets are the useful, desirable, and worthy aspects of your being—not based on someone else's evaluation, rather based on your own.

You are the only one who has the power to place real value on any aspect of yourself. You valuing self makes it real. Others only confirm what is already so, by simply recognizing your value, thus becoming attracted to you in some way.

It doesn't matter how many people see your value, if you are unable to appreciate it for yourself, then it does not exist. You will tend to behave in the manner of what you think about yourself. Therefore, the value you place on yourself will become evident to others.

We stumble in our progression when we don't take the time to discover what we really want. We strive hard to become a part in someone else's world, measuring our self-worth according to their scale. Each of us is a sun in our universe. We give permission to others to become a part of it.

Therefore, we must stop in our triviality and acquaint the world with the power we have within. Instead of seeking to borrow light from others, we are very capable of becoming projectors of the divine light—which comes from the Ultimate Self and is the definitive source of all light and life. Regardless of what our spiritual stand is and what path we choose, recognition of THE ONE, that Ultimate Source is an indicator showing signs of life.

There is no need to worry about "fitting in" or being "on time." "In" is relative and there is no such thing as "time." There is space. Where you are in terms of space, depends on your point of reference. If THE ONE is your point of reference, then you are "existing" in space and thus become unlimited and boundless.

Be that as it may, some people seem to choose to occupy space rather than to exist. Yet, occupying space is like describing life rather than living it. What a compulsive, limited, and potential state of being. Who really wants that way of life?

Kinetic energy is power and force in motion. We must strive to be kinetic energy, rather than potential energy. As we evolve into the person we were born to be, we prove indisputably that THE ONE is real. So we may as well stop attempting to fool ourselves into believing that we are not all of the beautiful things that we really are.

There's no need to live in someone else's image, see through someone else's eyes, hear through someone else's ears, and think someone else's thoughts. The Ultimate Self is that all-seeing, all hearing and all-knowing one. It is the "God" in you wanting to connect to the "God" in others. The Ultimate Self is THE ONE. So, it is always seeking to unite into ONENESS.

When a person knows what they have to offer and what they want to gain, it becomes ever so clear what must be done. This is the reason why it is so important early on, for us to assess our assets. When we measure the distance between the two points of our lives, we become inspired to start living and doing the things necessary to achieve greatness.

Assessing and being who you are is about experiencing the joy of living. It is about joyfully being yourself in all of your splendor, your magnificence, and beauty. Assessing and being you, is accepting THE ONE and THE ONE's creation – Which is YOU.

Assessing and being who you are, is about being in sync and alignment with the Ultimate Self—the only reality.

Chapter Two Monologue: Find the Power Within

Good morning my dearest friend. You have been the one closest to me and still here you are, even though I have not been good to you. I have turned away from you at every turn and fled your friendship even though I knew in my heart you were a loyal and trusting comrade. So grateful am I you have come to

Assessing and Being Who You Are

visit. Please, pardon my appearance. I am sick and very weak.

Yes, it's me. Lying here, not knowing whether I will live or die. This condition humbles me and forces me to see things in a different light. I realize I have been filled with pride and have been blinded by my own self-centeredness. I have tarried far too long, all the while knowing deep inside that you were my one true friend and helper. I have forsaken our friendship.

What you asked of me was a small request. We have been through so much together. I have most certainly grown as a result of our friendship. You've been patient and kind. You have sacrificed much for me. Yet, I took you for granted.

When I look at you, I am constantly reminded of what I should be. That is so hard for someone who sometimes gets full of himself. Okay, yes, I admit it! I have been a reluctant companion and have not shown much compassion for anyone else. Life may now swiftly leave me. So I presume this is my confession. Perhaps my weakness is because I have carried the burden of not taking responsibility for what is right and not being accountable for my own actions.

I have grown tired. I'm tired of running, tired of hiding, tired of not being what I know I should be. I am only running from myself. Looking into the quiet of my heart and mind, I know the truth. I have been a coward. Here you are proving your friendship once again.

Here I lay, while you pity me. Must you be so kind toward such a fool? I've ignored you and most of all, I have ignored myself and my own heart's calling.

In my hour of greatness, I stood tall and smug. My attitude of self-righteousness caused me to take the position of caring about only those things that mattered to me personally. I took a position that it's not worth doing things I don't want to do. I was content at how things were. I dreaded change. I was horrified of even the thought of change.

When you asked me to travel with you to that wretched place, and provide the people with opportunity, all I could think of was the amount of work, time and effort it would take. I just couldn't see myself being bothered with such ignorance and people who to me are nuisances. I became angry, and resented you for even suggesting we travel there.

"Be responsible."

"Be accountable."

"Do this..."

"Do that..."

Oh, God! I asked myself, "When will it ever stop?" The demands were too great. So, I did what any reasonable person might do. I disappeared. Yes, that's right. I left to keep from dealing with any hassles. I failed miserably. Pride kept me in a state of denial. My long time friend, haven't you figured it out yet? I'd rather do things my way and in my time.

Call me whatever names you like. I deserve it. I simply chose not to engage in those things that would cause me any discomfort. The task you wanted my assistance on was just too unbearable. Not to mention, the place where you wanted my company is such an insufferable place. Who would ever want to be there?

I resented being called a coward! I beg your pardon! I'm not a coward. Why should I be inconvenienced? It's absolutely not necessary to be troubled or weighed down unnecessarily. I most certainly prefer the simple life with simple delights. I was completely content. Why suffer me to such meaningless tasks?

You have all of these brilliant ideas, which usually means, more work for me! You should know me by now. Work never eludes me. Yet, it gratifies me to escape work that drains me of energy or binds me to things that really do not matter. And vagarious people appall me. They cause unnecessary strife and struggle in my life.

You see, it was prudent on my part to avoid them at all cost. Except this time, my running may have cost me my life. My affairs are in turmoil. I have ignored the things that needed my attention. The stress of it all has rendered me with grave pains in my heart.

I left that which was necessary and important. I have failed to nurture and give attention to my own. Consequently, I am experiencing probably the most devastating storm one could ever face. I can still hear those nagging voices in the back of my head!

"Stop wasting your life and time running from the best of yourself?"

"You have countless gifts, why don't you spend more time cultivating your God-given talents?"

"You have a higher calling on your life."

"Pride will ruin you."

"Stop being so self-centered."

Why would anyone want to hear such irritating and annoying chatter? I screamed perniciously at the souls who would dare persist in their assertions. Is this a curse? Tell me! I desperately plead of you, my friend. Am I cursed or being punished? Has God frowned upon me and turned His back on me? Is it too late for me? Have I wasted my life so that now I must give it up? I beg of you my trusted guide, answer me!

If only I could have just another chance to do it over again. I shall go with you. I shall forget about my life and dedicate it to help you. I shall focus on being a man of impeccable character. I shall cast out all fear and pride. I shall serve. I shall serve! I will come out of hiding. I will stand. I will stand! Did you hear me? I will stand! Please, help me! Please! Please! Will you help me to stand?

Life's Lesson:

We really don't become fulfilled, until we are able to do the things we enjoy doing and have a knack for doing.

It's natural to experience some anxiety about change. Nonetheless, as we start to focus on our needs by tapping into our gifts, change takes place gradually. As a result, we began to find success through many avenues. As we explore those avenues, we realize that a whole new world is opened up.

Words of Wisdom:

- ❖ No matter what life brings your way, hold your head up and face each day as a new beginning.

- ❖ Consider each day another chance of succeeding; always remembering that failure only exists when we don't try.

❖ No matter what obstacles are presented, keep going, keep working hard, stay focused, and don't give up!

WORKBOOK PART 2

Section I – Understanding the Personal SWOT Analysis

The SWOT Analysis Method: A SWOT Analysis is an effective tool used to evaluate Strengths, Weaknesses, Opportunities, and Threats. It is often used in business and some Life Coaches use it in Life Coaching. The SWOT analysis method helps you to look at yourself from a more objective point of view.

The premise behind this way of looking at things is a perspective which helps you to identify internal and external factors which impact successful outcomes for your life. Internal factors are your personal strengths and weaknesses; while the external factors deal with the opportunities and threats that might be presented by the external.

The four main questions to answer within the context of the SWOT process are:

1. How do I effectively utilize my strengths to be my best?

2. How do I eliminate my weaknesses and turn them into strengths?

3. How do I efficiently seize and maximize every opportunity presented to achieve my goals and objectives?

4. How do I strategically defend against threats to minimize harm to me?

This process can be very enlightening, get you started on the right track, and help you put your problems and challenges into proper perspective.

Observations & Thoughts
Journal your observations and thoughts here from Part 2, Section I

Section II – Analyzing Your Strengths

Answer the following questions thoroughly. The information is based on self-evaluation and analysis, not on evaluations or analysis from someone else's perspective.

1. What are your greatest Assets?

2. What advantages do you have that you believe others do not have?

3. What do you do better than anyone else that you know or have met?

4. What personal resources do you have access to or at your disposal?

5. What do others say your strengths are or you are good at doing?

6. What stands out about you the most?

Observations & Thoughts
Journal your observations and thoughts here from Part 2, Section II

Section III- Examining Your Weaknesses

Answer the following questions thoroughly. The information is based on self-evaluation, self-examination and analysis, not on evaluations or analysis from someone else's perspective.

1. What areas do you know that you need to improve upon?

2. What areas do you have fewer or no resources?

3. What areas cost you time, money and cause loss instead of create gains?

4. What areas are others likely to perceive as weaknesses?

5. What areas do others say you need to improve?

6. What area is important to you yet tends to get overlooked by others?

Observations & Thoughts
Journal your observations and thoughts here from

Section IV- Being Aware of What Threatens to You

Answer the following questions thoroughly. The information is based on self-evaluation, self-examination, awareness, and analysis, not on evaluations or analysis from someone else's perspective.

1. What circumstances exist in your environment that may harm you or become destructive to what you are working to achieve?

2. Who is your competition and what are they doing?

3. What threats and/or challenges do your weaknesses expose you to?

4. What environmental factors could hinder your growth and/or success?

5. What are you doing to protect yourself from that which threatens you?

6. What are you doing to overcome your weaknesses while minimizing your threats?

Observations & Thoughts
Journal your observations and thoughts here from Part 2, Section IV

Section V– Knowing What Opportunities Are at Hand

Answer the following questions thoroughly. The information is based on self-evaluation, self-examination, awareness, analysis, and paying attention to what is going on around you, not on evaluations or analysis from someone else's perspective.

What opportunities are open to you at the moment?

What trends can you take advantage of right now?

How can you turn your strengths into wonderful opportunities?

What are you currently doing to prepare yourself for when opportunities arise?

What areas are opportunities likely to come from?

What opportunities do you expect to come from the work that you are currently doing?

Opportunities – Observations & Thoughts
Journal your observations and thoughts here from
Part 2, Section V

༺༻

The largest and deepest mine is my own well of creativity. There is where I shall be very busy unearthing the most precious gems the world has yet to behold..

3

Learning to Love the You That You Discover

Loving yourself is a necessary step to loving others. Before you can grow to appreciate and love yourself, you must first come into the knowledge of who you are and your connection to the Ultimate Self. Only through a recognition of and proper relationship with the Ultimate Self are you able to accept yourself as you are at any given moment.

Once you travel through the many experiences that life can offer, you'll develop more of an appreciation and love for even some of the simplest of things. Authentic love starts with a connection to the Ultimate Self and the accomplishment of what you agreed to do in the context of that relationship. Some may refer to it as duty. Duty is that which you gave your word to fulfill. Thus, in the context of relationships, it is your word which makes you duty-bound, responsible, and accountable. True and authentic love is divine love. Divine love is based on principles carried into action on a consistent and continual basis.

Love is the ultimate law of the universe. It is inspiration in the creative process. Love is not simply an emotion that drives your impulses. It is decisive. To love is to live life. To love is to become one with THE ONE. In order to love completely, we must eliminate the vices of the world that we tend to grasp for fear of losing control.

In truth, are we really in control? While we may have some measure of it over our lives, do you believe that a power greater than yourself is the cause of your existence? If you believe this as I do, then we could concur that THE ONE is author of everything in existence. THE ONE is the Ultimate and is expressed through us. If you agree with this point, then don't you think that THE ONE is more than capable and qualified of being a guiding force in your life and to be intricately involved your affairs? I ask you to consider the following. What is THE ONE'S style of leadership? How does THE ONE guide us and how does THE ONE exercise authority in our lives?

I often think and meditate on this. The thoughts are triggered as I search my own innermost thoughts and beliefs. The understanding and evolution of my thoughts progress over time and evolve as I grow and become closer to my authentic self. It's easy to allow others to run interference in your life, causing you to submit to all sorts of foolishness and whims.

If we're not careful, we can get off course and lose track of what we want to do as a result of allowing others into our hearts in such a way that becomes destructive to our own sense of self and self-worth.

When I meditated on the above questions, I realized that THE ONE inspires me and draws me near with "loving-kindness." THE ONE recognizes the attractive qualities in each of us and maintains a sense of oneness with us. THE ONE is forgiving, warm-hearted, considerate and sympathetic to the point where there is an obvious expression of tenderness and gentleness.

Even in the subtle truths THE ONE makes us aware, and in those areas where correction is needed, it is revealed with the most profound mercy and beneficence. THE ONE is humane. There is an active demonstration of goodwill. Although, sometimes we may misinterpret the good for not being able to see through the pain and hardship that life can sometimes bring. Our ability to overcome and get to the other side of through is what helps us to be able to look back and see the magic in the process. Reflection allows us to see that magic after the fact. Mindfulness allows us to experience the magic in the moment.

When we surrender to the extraordinary power of THE ONE willfully, completely, and unhindered, we experience a multi-dimensional encounter. Consequently, we come to discover who we really are through a "love affair" with THE ONE, and fall completely and fully in love authentically. The love that stems from an authentic love, recognition, and appreciation of the relationship with THE ONE and self is what sets the tone and pace for love with others.

What does it mean to "surrender" to THE ONE willfully and completely? Who is THE ONE, to which you are surrendering? To willfully and completely surrender, is to voluntarily give of oneself entirely to the power of another, being undivided in cause and purpose.

It means to deliberately be uncompromising in relinquishing and/or yielding to the power of another without being forced or pressured. It is to intentionally give back every aspect or part of that which has been granted without obligation or the compulsion to do so.

THE ONE," is the author and Originator of your life, whose eternal spirit dwells within you. THE ONE is the Ultimate Self. THE ONE is the power existing deep within giving you the strength and fortitude to change your condition. The spirit within the essence of your being is the moral fiber, life energy, and character which comes alive when you operate within the realm of THE ONE'S energy field.

Plugging into this source allows you to understand love in a way never discovered because by "plugging" into it you are given a demonstration by THE ONE and a practical lesson which facilitates a deeper understanding of life and nature. The manifestation of divine love happens when we connect to our origin; and the origin starts with the essence of self, which is the Ultimate Self.

All things are possible when we operate within the circle of truth. The only time we lose control is when we let go of truth and hold on to vices. In reality, the vices are bad habits and practices that hinder us from unearthing our true selves, our authentic selves.

Why become overwhelmed with fear? The full experience of love is hindered when fear plagues you. Without love you are limited. Love allows you to bring into existence the universe within and affect the universe without. Everything we see is an expression of love. Yet, if your reality is anything other than peaceful, exciting, joyous and wonderfully magnificent, then you need to awaken the love within yourself. Perhaps, you may need to come alive.

Experiencing love is about knowing you, accepting you and being you. True love appreciates what is, and does not get caught up into what was. Divine love recognizes that everything is now, and now is continuous all the time. Real and authentic love appreciates, it attracts self, and generates the now experience into the future.

Burying yourself in excuses only causes you to stay stagnate. It may appear that you are moving, but are you really? Where are you going? Stop judging the self based on the past! Practice forgiving yourself, for what you have perceived to be mistakes. Move yourself out-of-the-way for forgiveness from the Ultimate Self. Grow to love you.

Know that everything that has entered into your atmosphere at some point was only a lesson of love. Remember though that love accepts what is, yet evolves and grows on a continual basis. Everything about you is created from love. Love is what it is – all of the time – it is love. Loving authentically is about loving yourself at every interval of change.

The science and art of meditation is a tool that helps one get in tune with the Ultimate Self. It is the process of going within the core of your being and aligning and balancing your energy centers. These hubs of power within are commonly referred to as wheels of light or chakras. During the process of meditation, you take yourself into a deeper state of relaxation and awareness with a single-point of reference. In other words, when you engage in meditation, you are actually setting yourself into a higher state of consciousness.

Meditation also allows you to clear the pathways for energy to flow and rotate throughout the body steadily and evenly. These pathways are often referred to as meridians. When energy is able to flow continuously throughout the body without hindrance, and the power points or chakras are able to effectively balance and control energy flow, we are then able to stabilize our bodies.

This actually protects us from dis-ease and other types of mental or spiritual attacks that cause destruction of our being. Meditation helps us to actively respond to that which is in contrary to good health and well-being.

In order to place yourself in a state of supreme happiness and ecstasy or as some say "place yourself in heaven at once," you must accept the commission to go within the heart of your soul with deliberate, purposeful intentions and with one single focus. Balance requires you to make straight all aspects of your internal self and to connect to the Ultimate Self, so that you clear the way for a higher state of awareness and consciousness. This is done only by going beyond the usual and reflexive/responsive "thinking" mind.

The word "meditate" in its root means "to measure." In order to measure effectively, it's important to bring everything about yourself into line or alignment. The key is to stay poised and keep upright. Keeping upright, on a straight course, or being authentic and truthful makes it easier to measure accurately. One is unable to make sound decisions when unable to measure accurately.

Learning to love the you—that you discover, is coming to an understanding that you were created in truth, and nothing else really exists other than truth. Even a liar is in truth a liar, and can be nothing else but what he/she is – a liar. That is the truth of the matter. So if you are internally out of sync with the truth of how and why you were even brought into existence, then you are not in line with truth.

In this instance you would be in violation of the principles of truth. I guarantee that there are external messages being sent, whether you receive them or not, that is a testament and bears witness to the fact that you are not in alignment, when not in line with your truth. You know why? All you have to do is examine what you are experiencing in your life now.

If what you are experiencing is not in sync with what you deeply feel in your soul of where you should be, then there is an inconsistency. The inconsistency is shown in your external environment when internal and external situations are not in harmony. The truth is spoken deep within your essence and if what you see externally is not consistent with your internal messages of truth then there is an imbalance.

Meditation is the pause needed to help you realign yourself and cultivate the love that is present within. Love is the central and fundamental component of the creative process and the creation of your "whole" self. Please understand that love is and has always been the most important part of your creation.

Love is the absolute truth. If you do not love yourself, then you have not discovered yourself yet. Love is the ultimate law of the universe. Everything comes into existence by this law – The Law of Love. When a person is living authentically, they love authentically. There is only ONE REALITY. There is a saying that goes, "God is Love." Under this precept, one could assert that to find the "God Within" is to find the "Love Within."

It is time to mine out those precious jewels. It is time to discover the hidden treasures buried far beneath your surface. Sure, you might find some things that appear to be worthless. Yet, know that everything in you is a necessary factor, and must be examined and analyzed very carefully and mindfully.

Even if what you find within becomes discarded or ultimately not used in the final product, nevertheless, it is necessary, if for no other reason than to understand that it was not needed in the first place. That particular knowledge and understanding only comes by going through the process.

Experiencing trials and struggles are part of the process of life and transformation. Just as a diamond is a precious stone, its beauty is recognized only after fire and pressure has been applied. We must learn to first accept the diamond in its unrefined state, which is coal. The fire and pressure facilitates the cultivation and perfection of coal into diamond. If you are unwilling to accept the coal, then you are unable to truly appreciate the diamond, for the diamond is the result of coal being put through the fire.

Did you know that coal comes from plants that were once alive? Plant remains were preserved by water and mud over spans of time. Through a process, the remains of plants and trees that died off were swamped over and buried underground for millions of years.

What we call "coal" contains energy that was in the plants when they were alive. After the plants died, the energy from the plants remained. This energy was transferred into coal, which was formed through a process over time, and is now used as fuel. As a result, coal was given the name, "fossil fuel". In order to get to coal, it takes a process of digging and mining it out of the ground. To get to a diamond is to continue the process until it reaches it stage of brilliance.

Your gifts, which were created in love, have always been a part of you. They will stay hidden and obscured from view until you make them known. The energy that was deposited within you, regardless of your present state or condition, remains within, waiting to be transferred into your conscious awareness and used to secure benefit for you, your family, and the world. As long as you do not recognize your gifts, mine them out and put them to use, they remain dormant and unrefined. Furthermore, you deprive yourself, your family and the world of something truly remarkable.

Like coal, we must go through a process of transformation. Our gifts must not be left alone, rather given the attention necessary to use them for what they were intended. Awaken to the knowledge and awesome power of love. Get up and live! There is so much for you to do. SMILE.

Can a diamond exist without fire and pressure? Can you become your best self without trials and struggle? The secret to the diamond lies within the coal. Likewise the secret to extraordinary living lies within the seemingly ordinary things about you. You have gifts.

Discover what they are and grow to love you for who you are and who you have the power to become. Appreciate yourself and others even in the unrefined state. You may not understand who you are now. You may not even appreciate who you are now. Yet, love self now, not for who you are now, but for who you have the potential to become.

Love is THE ONE, and THE ONE is not only limited to now. THE ONE is eternal and always THE ONE. When one is eternal, they exist. In order to exist, one must be in motion. THE ONE is always in motion and always in the creative process.

Although you may not be at your highest state of existence, you have the potential to become the extraordinary human being that you were born to be. Continue to grow, while loving yourself at every stage of growth. Love recognizes the potential. Love, loves self for love's potential, and is always loving and accepting who and what love is. Love is what it is – Y-O-U, living life in love.

Chapter Three Monologue: Arise and Come Forth!

What voice is this that harkens in the darkness? A familiar sound indeed, but how could it be when I am here alone? The sweetest sound to thine own ears is the call of a man's name. Yet, this must be an appeal emerging from the depths of my imagination. No soul lies here with me in this hollow grave and no stimulation lurks to cultivate the buried gift that has died with me. So, who are you and whence have you come, calling, "Arise! Get up! Live!"

Stranger in the night, these are certainly peculiar words you speak, because I am alive. And just as I am speaking now, I am alive. Yes! It is true, I have lost the desire to toil and press on because my efforts have been met with such opposition and difficulty. Every imaginable and foreseen stumbling block has been placed in my path, and my labor has seemed useless, worthless and has bore no fruit. It seems pointless to continue in this vain course while at every turn I have been ineffective. I have failed!

I have become dull and lowly from this grave in which I have fallen. This pitiful condition is where the weight of my problems and worries has weighed me down to the point of becoming the greatest burden of all. I have descended into a pit of shame. The overwhelming trials and obstacles lie in wait to ambush me even as I attempt to stand. I lack luster and now dwell in a place that is vile and inferior. And every miserable and heartbroken wretch seeks pleasure in my company, while I despise theirs.

Here am I, alone, in the dark and weary night of my life. Disillusioned and disenfranchised. Disappointed and dissatisfied. I am fed up, worn out, worn down and just tired of this battle to nowhere. From whence shall my help come? When shall I be delivered from this cycle of non-productivity, this cycle of working, but making no progress? How is it that I'm exerting large amounts of energy, but am realizing no improvements in my condition? Why is it that I have nothing to show for my efforts? Is my labor in vain?

Yes, you call my name. Who are you? And why now have you come? For an eternity, I have been praying for a worthy companion – one who would stand beside me, to love me, support me, and transform my dark world into a light burning with passion, enthusiasm and zest. For days, I have yearned for one to help shape my smallest idea into a vision that comes to life with a gentle word of comfort and encouragement. Today, I have petitioned the Almighty to show me an example that I may pattern myself after until such time I am able to stand and be that example.

Companion - Arouse me with the sound of your voice! Light the fire in my soul! Example - stand strong and tall, let me see you. If you are real, come out of the dark and show me who you really are. My bones are shaking, as I am about to thrust forth from this grave of loneliness and despair. Someone, and yet another has called out to me. "Arise! Wake up. Come forth!"

My heart is beating once again from the rhythm of your call. You have stirred the gift within me. Yet, who is this calling, when it is only me here in this shallow grave? What dares to inspire such a motionless creature? Can it be my own thoughts echoing in this dark place and vibrating back to my consciousness? No one else is in here with me; yet, I am here – unseen and unknown. You say, "Come forth, come forth!" How humiliating and disgraceful to bring out in the open such a one who is small-minded, one-dimensional and silly. I've ignored all signs of life around me? Must I let the world see how trifling, superficial and insignificant I have been?

You say, "Wake up!" If I have been asleep, today I am alert and stand ready to come forth. Help me to grow. Assist me in promoting my truest and more honorable self. Teach me how to build up, expand and increase my value. "Get up, you say?" I am up. Where I once was inactive, idle and slow-moving, I hear your command to "Arise!" I hear you! I hear you calling my name and here I stand diligent, attentive, spirited, dynamic and full of life.

At last, it's me, beholder of the visitor in the darkness of night. Here stands a witness of the star of piercing brightness, who guarded my soul ever so carefully, and brought me forth from death unto life.

My gift once again lives, and that which was buried and hidden within, is now exposed!

Life's Lesson:

In life we face many challenges. These trials help to build character. If change is desired, it doesn't matter where to begin as much as it does just beginning. It doesn't matter how many times we have to start, the key is starting.

Set goals in your life. Sometimes a change in environment can mark a fresh start. Sometimes, even a change in association is the necessary space needed to grow.

Words of Wisdom:

❖ Procrastination is the most utilized excuse for the fearful, and the most consistent activity of the lazy.

- ❖ A dream is a hope in the dark; a vision is the reality, when we have awakened.

- ❖ Recreate yourself daily, otherwise you will look back and realize that nothing has really changed in your life.

- ❖ Love is, no matter what. Authentic Love is when you live your truth.

WORKBOOK PART 3

Section I – Self Discovery

Directions for Completing the Exercise: This exercise is designed to help you look at yourself very closely and mine out the beauty that lies within. First, get into a quiet place where you will not be disturbed. Allow at least an hour for this particular exercise. Once in the quiet space where you will not be disturbed, next take out a hand mirror, and spend ten (10) minutes looking at yourself in the mirror.

Use the entire ten (10) minutes looking at yourself and into your own eyes. Avoid looking away. Look carefully into the depths of your eyes. Examine every aspect of your bone structure, your lips, and your face. After you have done this for a full ten (10)

Learning to Love the You That You Discover 105

minutes, put the mirror down for a moment, and answer the questions outlined here in Section I. Pick up the mirror if you get stuck on a question or need to remind yourself of what you saw.

- ❖ When you look at yourself deeply, who do you see?

- ❖ When you look into the mirror, do you like the person you see? Why or why not?

- ❖ When you look at yourself deeply, what do you see?

- ❖ When you look into the mirror, do you like the things you see? Why or why not?

- ❖ As you looked deeply into your eyes, what did your eyes tell you about the person that was staring back at you in the mirror?

- ❖ As you looked deeply at the person in the mirror, what did you feel?

- ❖ As you looked deeply at the person in the mirror, what did you think?

- ❖ As you examined the person in the mirror, what questions went through your mind?

- ❖ As you examined carefully the person in the mirror, what ten (10) things would you offer him/her if they came to you for guidance?

- ❖ As you felt the depth of the person during examination, what ten (10) things would you say to help him/her be their very best?

Observations & Thoughts
Journal your observations and thoughts here from Part 3, Section I

Section II – Getting to Know Yourself Better

Answer the following questions thoroughly. The information is based on self-awareness and you taking the time to look within and ask yourself questions that you might not have asked or thought of before now. The series of questions are not based on someone else or what others think about you. They are questions for you to consider without another person's influence. Be open and honest with yourself. There is no wrong or right answer. It just is what it is! SMILE.

WHAT'S IN A NAME

- ❖ What is your full name?
- ❖ What does your name mean?
- ❖ Who named you?
- ❖ Do you like your name? Why or why not?

- ❖ Have you ever thought of changing your name? Why or why not?

- ❖ If you thought of changing your name, what would you change it to?

- ❖ What is it about that name that appeals to you?

- ❖ If you were your mother, what would you have named you when you were born, why?

COLORS OF THE WORLD

- ❖ What is/are your favorite color(s)?

- ❖ What is it about the color(s) that attracts you?

- ❖ Where do you find yourself using this color the most?

- ❖ Who or what does the color remind you of?

- ❖ When you are happy, what color(s) come to mind?

- ❖ When you are sad, what color(s) come to mind?

- ❖ When you are sexually aroused, what color(s) come to mind?

- ❖ When you are turned off or put off, what color(s) come to mind?

- ❖ When you are angry, what color(s) come to mind?

- ❖ When you are afraid, what color(s) come to mind?

- ❖ When you are embarrassed, what color(s) come to mind?

- ❖ When you are excited, what color(s) come to mind?

- ❖ Write a story, poem, or song as you see the world using the colors you described above?

- ❖ Discuss how you can make your world better using the colors you described above under the categories of sad, turned off or put aside, angry, afraid, embarrassed?

- ❖ Recount a funny story of a time in your life using the colors you described previously under the categories of happy, sexually aroused, and excited.

LIKES AND DISLIKES

- ❖ What is your favorite food?

- ❖ What is it about that food that you like besides its taste?

- ❖ What is your least favorite food?

- ❖ What is it about that food that you dislike besides its taste?

- ❖ What is your favorite part of your body?

- ❖ What is it about that part of your body that you like?

- ❖ What is your least favorite part of your body?

- ❖ What is it about that part of your body that you dislike?

- ❖ What is your favorite day of the week and why?

- ❖ What is your least favorite day of the week and why?

- ❖ What is your favorite activity and why?

- ❖ What is your least favorite activity and why?

- ❖ What is your favorite quote or phrase and why?

- ❖ What is your least favorite quote or phrase and why?

- ❖ What is your favorite name, why?

- ❖ What is your least favorite name, why?

- ❖ What is your number one like and dislike of all time?

Number One Like:

Number One Dislike:

LOVING YOURSELF

Using the letter of your name, use words to describe yourself. For example: ATIYA (artistic, tenacious, intelligent, youthful, amicable).

- ❖ List Your Name:

- ❖ List Words That Describe YOU!

- ❖ Now Define Those Words!

- ❖ Taking into account the descriptive words above, and an understanding of their meaning, write a description of yourself. Start out with the phrase, "My name is…"

- ❖ List twenty-four (24) things you like.

- ❖ List twenty-four (24) things you love about yourself.

HOPES, DREAMS, AND SPIRITUAL THINGS

- ❖ What are your spiritual beliefs, why?

- ❖ Describe your relationship with a higher force and how it impacts your daily living and decisions in life.

- ❖ What gives you the greatest joy in life?

- ❖ What brings you the most comfort?

- ❖ What helps you to relax and help you to wind down?

- ❖ What is success to you and what helps you to determine whether or not you have reached success in your life?

Observations & Thoughts
Journal your observations and thoughts here from Part 3, Section II

ೞେ

The knowledge of self is the first step on the ladder of success. No matter who you know or how much you know, you'd do well to know yourself.

4

Exercising Your Power to Be

Your power is veiled far beneath the surface of the Ultimate Self. As you uncover the hidden qualities, you will find that there is much more to yourself than you ever thought or imagined. When you become acquainted with your potential, your ability to create becomes greater than ever before. The force and energy contained within your very being comes alive to enable you to bring your ideas into existence.

When a thought or idea comes to your mind, certain conditions are favorable to make something remarkable happen. However, unless you do something about the thought that entered into your mind, your idea remains only an idea. This is an example of potential energy. While your mind may be positioned or fixed in a certain direction, unless you follow through and make movements in the direction of your mind, then you will only have the potential to go in that direction, rather than actually going there.

On the contrary, when you take the necessary steps to act upon a thought or idea that comes to your mind, and begin to do or produce what you imagine, you not only have the potential to do it, you actually do it. This is kinetic energy - energy that is in motion. Energy that is in motion is active energy. When you are active in your life, your activity has an amazing impact on others outside of yourself. Therefore to be involved in positive activities significantly changes the world for the better. Your constructive behavior produces phenomenal results and becomes a force on others around you. SMILE. Whether you see it or not, or understand it or not, you are very relevant.

You have the potential to become extraordinary. This power is innately positioned inside of you. It has always been there, waiting to be applied in your life. While this power is already within, if you do not produce actual results and effects, then you will still only have the potential. The aim is to move beyond having only potential to actually becoming and being living proof of who and what you are - extraordinary. This is what is meant by, exercising your power to be.

Exercising your power is to exert yourself physically and mentally for the sake of improving your condition. It is the process by which you put forth action and make use of all of your abilities to move in an upward direction to becoming the real you – the "I AM". Exercising your power to be is to be courageous in living your truth regardless of who thinks otherwise. The key to exercising this power is to connect to the essence of self – The Ultimate Self. Now, this is the origin or source of this energy that we call kinetic.

Examine a light bulb. What do you see? Some may perceive a complicated scientific experiment that led to an invention, which proved useful in these modern times. Others may wonder or marvel at the "genius" behind the invention. Many have become quite dependent upon this gadget containing many components. But, the fact of the matter is that, it was constructed by someone like you.

In order to get the ultimate and intended result from a light bulb, it must be connected to another source. Linking it to that other source, takes a being, like you, to connect it or it does not work. So no matter how incredible the light bulb may be, alone it is useless and only has the "potential" to convert electrical energy into visible light.

Look around and behold the manifestation of your power and greatness. Everything you set your eyes on came from you. Further still, you are far greater than all what's around you. To effectively use the power we have internally, we must stay plugged into the source that contains all power. It is within each of us. Most certainly it is within you too!

The creative process is sparked by a thought. Your ideas are the beginning of the making of your reality. The creative thought in your mind comes from inspiration, and inspiration only comes from the Creator. Thus, creativity comes from inspiration and the immediate influence of THE ONE. Creativity is when the Creator "breathes" into you and influences you with an idea or purpose. Test it! When you get an idea, ask yourself what is the source of inspiration.

Meditate on the circumstances surrounding that creative thought.

It is critically important to cultivate your natural gifts, which by the way are actually supernatural when cultivated. Likewise, it's essential to develop the great ideas that come to your mind. When you neglect your gifts and do not develop the ideas, your creative power diminishes because it is not being exercised.

Sure, it's there, but it's not being put to use. If you have not discovered what your natural gifts and talents are, it is because you are not reflecting and looking within. You have a gift. It is time to discover what your gifts are.

What sense does it make for a painter to buy all of the tools necessary to paint a beautiful picture, but never use them to actually paint the picture? What good then are the tools? What sense does it make for someone who wants to paint a picture, to let the idea of what they want to paint, be a fleeting one? Why would a painter who desires to paint a particular picture, not actually attempt to paint the picture in his mind first?

Taking the time and placing attention on bringing your idea or concept into existence takes effort and work. However, when you labor to produce something tangible, concrete, touchable from a mental picture, you actually manifest the power of THE ONE. Think about it.

An impression is made upon your mind as a result of various sets of circumstances. The spirit of inspiration breathes into the darkness of your mind. You take note of the idea and bring it forward to your conscious awareness and into focus, after which you then put forth effort and exert energy to bring the idea into a physical manifestation or otherwise into the light.

Those who see the material and evident achievement are usually not aware that the idea was in the making for a while. They often do not look deep into the creative process to truly understand the beauty of its manifestation. Thus, some successes are viewed as overnight sensations when in actuality success happened by way of a magical process that for the most part went undetected by those not involved in the creative process of it.

What we want to do at this junction is call attention to the process of creation. There is a saying, "There's magic in the process." Some may prefer to say there are miracles in the process. Either way, incredible things happen from the point of an idea to the point of manifesting it in real time. During the creative process – that moment life is conceived in your mind and heart, is the most profound and life-changing moment. In other words, from the beginning of conception to the final product of giving birth to an idea, astonishing things are taking place.

The key is to pay close attention to the process that is taking place. Pay close attention to the point when no one outside of yourself can comprehend what is happening. Sometimes even you are not consciously aware of the miracle that is being performed. Yet, if you pay close attention to your internal messages of truth, you will become aware of something very, very special.

The act of creation is feminine in expression. Anytime a good idea is conceived and intended to come forth, your mind and heart serves as a womb of THE ONE and a safe place to carry it for an appointed term. This vision is nurtured and eventually you give birth to something wonderful.

The mind and heart protect it, nurtures it and brings it to life. Just as a mother protects her child in the womb, nurtures it and ultimately gives birth, so it is in this regard. At the appropriate time, the idea is brought to light and made manifest to others. Yet, the brilliance of the new creation happened over time in the dark. It was present, yet obscured from view, being tended to without immediate observation.

The act of creating something tangible in your life starts with a marriage between the self and Ultimate Self. It is impossible to create anything outside of yourself without first recognizing the power that lies within. The Ultimate Self is the first act of creation, and then you are called into existence. None of us can be whole until we first recognize that our completeness is in the Ultimate Self – the real force and power that is within.

We have the tools necessary to paint our picture. However, our incompleteness is a result of needing to exercise force and power. We do this by operating within the scope and purpose of why we were born into the world. In other words, do what you have been born to do.

Exercising your power is cultivating and using the gifts and talents that are contained within your very makeup. Paint that beautiful and colorful picture. Compose a resplendent illustration containing the richest of hues. You are capable of doing that. Look within to mine out what is there.

Live your life graciously being alive and redefining yourself according to inspiration. Exercise the power to define yourself not based on how others see you, but define yourself based on who you truly are and the inspiration that comes from THE ONE. You can do it, you must do it, and you will do it.

Your gifts and talents are the keys to unlocking the door of paradise, bliss and ultimate happiness in this dimension here on Earth. Dig deep, pull out those keys and use them to walk through an extraordinary experience.

Chapter Four Monologue: The Woman From Tekoa

Your excellence, my most esteemed King David; I am most honored to be in your presence. I come clothed to appear as if I am in mourning. In truth, my beloved, I am here as a call from the Holy Spirit to bring you solace and peace of mind. I shall for your rest, comfort, most heartfelt prayer, and by the Almighty's permission who has heard your petition, use the ability to channel my God-given talent for a greater good to relieve you from your most tragic dilemma.

If I present myself to you as a widowed woman, whose husband has died, and her only two sons fought in the field with no one there to break it up, resulting in one killing the other, you would be most obliging and sympathetic, for you have a heart after God. If I enlightened you of the extenuating circumstances causing my entire family to raise up against me and demand of me to hand down my only living son so that he too may be put to death for murdering his brother, I know in my heart that you would be most gentle and kind as to assure me the protection of my son.

Thus, my beloved King, I absolve all fear and stand here with great courage before you and your Royal Court, to confront you boldly and in truth using every imaginable gift that the Almighty One has bestowed upon me. How can you in my case objectively judge the set of circumstances, yet fail to extend the same care to your own son? With all due respect Your Excellence, how dare you carefully and diligently guard me and my spirit, but refuse to be a keeper of your own soul?

How can you not suitably evaluate your own condition in a more impartial and balanced way? How can you not ease your own heart and mind and rid yourself of misery by bringing your exiled son back home? This story I have given you is but a fabrication to help you, my dearest King David, look into the mirror and see more clearly.

I am a woman from Tekoa that blessed city south of Bethlehem. I bring you fruit from my native land. Tis, I give you olive oil that you may be anointed in the midst of your troubles. I offer you but good and wise counsel from your Lord. I have been called from my place of comfort at the beckoning of He who loves you and I have most dutifully responded to the Beneficent's call.

I am a good woman. I am come with a clear work from God. My strength and character is derived from my fidelity to God. I am committed to doing that which is honorable at all costs, and this, my Beloved King David supersedes any amount of fear that I might have had in risking my life and presenting myself unto your throne. If my imagination shall be punished, then do with me what you will. I have done what God has commanded of me in this charge. I have done that which I have been required to do.

So I beg of you, as I bow and prostrate before your throne, not negating my loyalty to the Almighty, but in reverence and awe to Him who has given you your heart. "Please, help Oh, King." If any punishment must befall anyone, I say to you with a beam that you most surely see, "Let me be responsible for the sin, Your Majesty. Let my father's family be held responsible. Your Majesty and your throne are innocent."

Though I come as if I am in mourning, in truth, I only grieve, my Beloved King David, because of your state of affairs. "Help me, oh, King." Help me by guarding your own soul and by acting upon the inspiration to recall your son. He is most surely a product of you. Exercise your power for the sake of improving your own condition. God shall not change your condition, my beloved King, until you first move to change it yourself.

Life's Lesson:

Inside of every human being is the potential to be phenomenally great. There is a passion that burns deep within each of us which is the key to having meaning, happiness and fulfillment in our lives. This burning desire is the spark that existed from the beginning of our conception – that magical moment that THE ONE experienced when we were only a concept. When you were only a thought in the

Creator's mind, your purpose for being was also a part of that vision.

As THE ONE put forth action to make an idea manifest into something tangible – Y-O-U, there was an impartation (transmission) of an impression of THE ONE upon your heart and mind. As we reflect on why we have been born and our true purpose in life, we actually go through a preparatory process of joining and binding ourselves to our Creator. Preparation is the process of making our minds ready to receive inspiration from on high.

Reflection is the "act" of turning our thoughts back to our beginning or origin.

Our origin is THE ONE; and the gifts bestowed upon us are there for us to fully experience this incredible journey. Therefore, we must look within ourselves to discover our natural gifts and talents. Then, we must work to develop them and put them to use for our benefit and the benefit of others. This is what makes them supernatural or extraordinary.

Words of Wisdom:

- ❖ When we employ ourselves around the things we enjoy doing the most, we usually discover a gift and ultimately find happiness.

- ❖ We compromise our integrity when we do not use our gifts.

- ❖ A gift is THE ONE's way of showing us that we are loved. As proof and verification of that glorious and authentic love, THE ONE gives a part of that ultimate power to us. How we use our gifts demonstrates our love for THE ONE and manifests that Glory in us.

- ❖ Show me a man who does what he was born to do, and I will show you a man who believes in the power and reality of THE

ONE.

❖ To be a product of authentic love and light is to walk in your purpose.

WORKBOOK PART 4

Section I – ABC's of Success

Directions for Completing the ABC's of Success Chart: The Chart helps you to put in perspective your view of success. If you want to be successful, it is advantageous to outline what success looks like to you in order to be able to measure your progress.

This chart helps you to organize your concept of success in a visible and tangible format. In each category, list attitude, behavior, and character traits which you view to be characteristics of a person who is successful. Then at the end of the chart describe the characteristics of a successful person.

Remember to list what YOU believe to be true, not someone else's perspective of what success looks like. THIS IS ABOUT YOU! Pull out a sheet of paper and draw a box as shown labeled The ABC's of Success. Then proceed as outlined naming the Attitude, Behavior, Character Traits, and finally the Characteristics of a Successful Person.

The ABC's of SUCCESS		
ATTITUDE TRAITS	**BEHAVIOR TRAITS**	**CHARACTER TRAITS**
CHARACERISTICS OF A SUCCESSFUL PERSON		

Based on the above chart and a self-assessment, what attitudes, behaviors, and character traits are necessary for you to acquire in order to encompass the above success traits?

Observations & Thoughts
Journal your observations and thoughts here from Part 4, Section I

Section II- The Synergy Quadrant

In this section, you will need to create a personal synergy quadrant. This is a coaching tool I developed to help you frame your plan of action. First, get out a blank 8 ½ x 11 white sheet of paper. On the paper draw four even circles: two at the top and two more right underneath those two. You should have four identical circles on the page. Once you have done that, divide each circle into eight parts (like a pie chart).

Once that's complete, label the top left circle "Circle of Dreams." These are the things you want to accomplish in your life. Now, label the top right circle, "Circle if Impact." These are the areas of life that have an impact on what you do. Label the third circle located at the bottom left of your page, "Circle of Influence." These are the people who are intricately involved in your life and who influences your decisions. The last circle, located at the bottom right should be labeled, "Circle of Need." These are the things you need in order to accomplish your dreams, goals, and aspirations. Once you have completed creating your personal synergy quadrant as described above, follow the instruction in the next paragraph for completing it.

Complete the Synergy Quadrant. When completing it, avoid rushing through this exercise. Take your time and be very intentional. The Synergy Quadrant lays a foundation to firmly establish you toward the direction of your goals and objective. Complete every section. Use additional paper if necessary.

See How the Synergy Quadrant Should Look in the Example.

Create your own, labeling each quadrant section: Circle of Dreams, Circle of Impact, Circle of Influence, and Circle of Need.

This is a very resourceful tool to organize your thoughts for strategic planning processes.

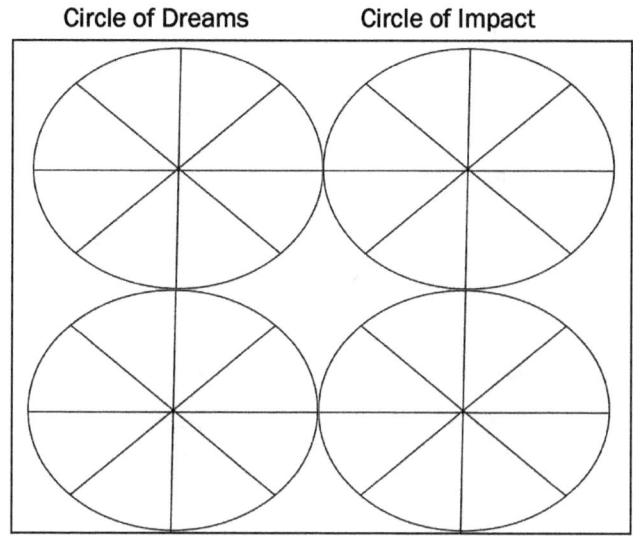

Circle of Dreams   Circle of Impact

Circle of Influence   Circle of Need

Observations & Thoughts
Journal your observations and thoughts here from Part 4, Section II

Section III – Building Your System of Support

Build your system of support. First, take out a plain white sheet of paper. Draw a small circle in the middle of the paper. Inside of that circle write the word, "ME." Once you have done that, draw eight more small circles of the same size around the circle labeled "ME." Now, draw lines from the "ME" circle to each of the other circles. It should look like spokes on a bicycle tire.

Once you have done that, place the names of those on your support team in each circle below. Make sure that these are people who want to see you succeed and who are willing to invest time in your success by mentoring, being a sounding board, or sharing information.

Refer to this chart often, and change names as needed. However, this is your support team, utilize it effectively.

Observations & Thoughts
Journal your observations and thoughts here from Part 4, Section III

Section IV- "I AM" 100%

List 100 positive things about yourself beginning with the phrase, "I AM…." Complete this exercise fully. YES YOU CAN think of 100 wonderful things about yourself, so no excuses!

Remember to start with "I AM…."

KEEP GOING! You can do it!
Remember to start with "I AM…."

DON'T YOU DARE STOP! You can do it! Keep Going. Remember to start with "I AM…."

KEEP GOING! You are almost there. Remember to start with "I AM…."

GREAT JOB! I told you it could be done! Now, what is the title of this section? (Say it aloud)

Observations & Thoughts
Journal your observations and thoughts here from Part 4, Section IV

☙❧

Self-discovery is one of the most fascinating
adventures one can embark upon.

5

Keeping Your Eyes on the Prize

Anytime we start something that we have purposed to do, there is excitement and zeal. We thrust forward with a whole lot of energy, and no one can keep us from accomplishing our goal. However, as soon as the first sign of trouble or a challenge comes our way, some of us turn back. Starting a life-changing journey is no different. The stakes are usually higher and the price even greater. So, I ask now, will you turn back or will you stay the course?

When a life-changing journey is intended, it's necessary to prepare yourself for the long haul. Staying the course requires tenacity, self-determination, and amazing will-power. It also requires a total commitment and a mind of perseverance. No matter how difficult the journey may be at the moment or becomes along the way, you have to have a stick-to-attitude and the belief that you can accomplish what you have set out to do. It may be difficult to endure the obstacles that are presented. Yet, if you prepare properly and are committed to keep going there is no reason why you are unable to be successful.

Although struggle happens when working to accomplish something worthy, preparation helps you to put yourself in proper condition or readiness for the undertaking you are embarking upon. Putting yourself in proper condition entails setting your mind and firmly fixing your intentions to complete the task at hand. Preparation calls for you to completely make up your mind to accomplish the assignment and to cut off whatever is necessary in order to be successful. Being prepared and making a commitment goes far beyond simply saying that I am going to do this or do that.

To commit, is to emotionally and morally engage. When one emotionally and morally engages, they become involved with, bind themselves to and hold fast to that which they are committed. Further, they attach their feelings and emotions to the matter and shape their behavior in a practical and applicable way as to not weaken the bond to that which they have committed.

Commitment deals with being active about something in particular with a pre-determined temperament, character and manner. Commitment is in fact energy in motion with a fixed and intended destination or outcome and result. One is unable to prove their intention on a matter without the declaration of demonstration in their behavior.

When it is said that, "commitment deals with being active about something with a pre-determined temperament, character, and manner," what is meant is that before the desired outcome is known or realized, the person has made an asserted commitment. They have committed and firmly established in their mind and heart that they will remain constant, faithful, trustworthy, attached, unwavering, resolved and firm in their decision to achieve what they intended or purposed to do.

In addition, a person who is committed will establish habits in thought and deed, and maintain a natural disposition to achieve those qualities that determines the nature of that which they are aiming to achieve. They stand firmly on their decision, and make adjustments when and where necessary in order to adhere to principles that will keep them fixed in the direction of their goal. They remain steadfast and their behaviors are characterized by good faith to achieve the stated goal or objective.

The process to committing to a goal can be likened to the process of marriage. In marriage, a husband and wife make a life-long commitment. They vow to forsake all others and stay faithful and loyal to one another until they are separated by death.

They vow that regardless of the circumstances, they will stay together. It goes something like this…"to have and to hold, from this day forward, for better, for worse, for richer, for poorer, in sickness or in health, to love and to cherish 'till death do us part. And hereto I pledge you my faithfulness."

During the course of marriage, the couple may be faced with a variety of challenges. Further, they may be confronted with matters, which will require them to make some very difficult decisions. In marriage, making a commitment requires them, as outlined in the vows, to forsake all others, and sometimes the decisions that may need to be made can be very painful.

Some decisions can be very difficult, yet to forsake all others means to give up, refuse, deny, decline, or leave altogether. Within the context of the commitment in marriage, anything that threatens or weakens the bond between husband and wife; causes abandonment or isolation of one spouse from the other; jeopardizes the unity of the couple; robs husband and/or wife of marital bliss, peace or joy; causes unnecessary friction or is a nuisance; or anything else that becomes a threat to the longevity and success of the marriage, must be re-evaluated and a firm decision made with respect to that which is causing the threat for harm to exist.

The marriage becomes priority due to the commitment made. The aim or objective is for the couple to stay together. However, in staying together, a focus must also be on keeping the marriage relationship in the same or better condition as when it first began.

In order to achieve the goal intended for the marriage, both husband and wife must heavily incline toward one another. They must create habits of mind and adhere to practices which preserves the marriage, protects it against attack, and supports its continued existence. Also, both husband and wife must make adjustments when and where necessary in order to adhere to principles that will keep them fixed in the direction of their goal – A life-long marital commitment and marital bliss.

A couple's tendencies, activities, responses, actions and circumstances must be in accordance with honesty, trust, sincerity, fairness, lawfulness of purpose, and absent of any intent to defraud or act maliciously. Their relationship must be clear of behaviors that are harmful and injurious; otherwise it is characterized as abuse and abuse, physical or otherwise, makes it very difficult to sustain a marriage.

Abuse is improper and gross misuse of the marriage relationship. It must be eliminated immediately because it undermines and attacks the very core of the marriage threatening the life of the marriage and the two people in the marriage relationship. A marriage is unable to thrive when abuse exists, whether it is physical, verbal, emotional, or mental.

When an abusive situation occurs, it must be immediately corrected. Abusive behavior creates an unhealthy environment and compromises the integrity of the marriage. When it continues to exist and is not corrected, the decision to leave the marriage may be the only alternative, and this too can be a very painful decision.

Staying the course with respect to any goal is possible. It may sometimes be tough, but it's possible. Your desire to attain your goal must be greater than the challenges that may come up as you are working to reach it. Keeping your focus might sometimes seem like an impossible feat, especially as obstacles arise. However, although it is not always easy to achieve something of value, you can achieve what you will, just continue pressing on until you reach the mark!

Reaching or "hitting the mark" takes a whole lot of target practice and a lot more charisma. SMILE. Charisma is that little "extra" that makes ordinary extraordinary. Charisma is a very rare quality that gives a person influence and arouses in others a sense of dedication, commitment, and enthusiasm. It is an extremely favorable quality and gift to have. With charisma comes extraordinary power and favor that exudes grace, personal charm, beauty and kindness.

It is exhilarating to observe one who has a charismatic persona. A person of this type of distinction may rejoice in being able to exercise the power to summon the greatest forces in the universe to submit to a worthy and relevant cause. My favorite description of what charisma is and how it works is this… "Charisma is 'having the ability to overcome competing forces for the greater good.'"

There are competing forces that present themselves when you work to attain something of consequence. While you are fortunate to know exactly what you are after and while the product of your creation is something to celebrate, sustaining the ability to keep your eye on the prize during the process will prove to be one of your greatest accomplishments. Overcoming competing forces is an accomplishment indeed!

Keeping Your Eyes on the Prize

Have you ever noticed that when you set out to do something how many other conflicting opportunities come your way? When you have made a decision to accomplish a goal, have you ever gotten the feeling that you were being tempted by someone or something that could interfere with your time or take your attention away from your decision to do something else? Most likely the answer is yes!

Along the way, we may be tempted with things, which could entice us to stray from our intended path, hindering our ability to achieve what we set out to accomplish. However, our success depends on our strength to resist temptation. Can you imagine the devastation in a marriage if either the husband or wife or both were unable to resist temptation? Well, the same is true on the journey to achieving anything great.

Opportunities will come our way to help us move closer to our goals. Other or perceived opportunities may come as a result of forces that operate naturally within the universe to challenge us. When we form the necessary habits of mind and maintain that natural disposition as discussed earlier, we will automatically incline toward our goal. In fact, we will become stronger in our resolve.

The struggle it takes to maintain a natural inclination is what actually "works us out" and "gets us in shape" to reach a healthy balance with respect to our conduct. Consistency in our efforts is very important. The consistency of our actions and responses to situations develops character and helps us to reach a level of excellence over time which ultimately determines the outcome or the integrity of the product we bring forth.

Although a couple may be able to withstand and stay together in spite of challenges that come their way, the quality or condition of the marriage is predicated on necessary behavior changes that keep threatening issues from remaining a problem in the marriage. Full commitment is based on completing the goal and protecting the integrity of the process. If both of these areas are not met, then no real and total commitment has been made. Further, a full commitment is evidence of adequate preparation, and without preparation, it is impossible for one to fully commit.

Any goal, whether it be marriage, starting a business, writing a book, implementing a program or losing weight, requires both preparation and total commitment, and in that order. Again, preparation is the process of putting yourself in proper condition or readiness to start the task. It's also cutting off those things that could hinder you from accomplishing your goal.

Total commitment involves engaging and making use of every aspect of your being in the process of accomplishing what it is you want to accomplish. It is keeping your eyes fixed and unwavering on the task in order to complete it. Just saying I will do this or do that isn't enough. Preparation and a total commitment is what will ensure that you will keep your eyes fixed on the prize.

Being adequately prepared, totally committed and keeping your eyes on the prize is great, but there is something else that needs consideration? The universe is going to test the integrity of your intentions. As you become even more focused on accomplishing your goals, you will find that more and more people will attempt to divert your attention away from what you are doing. This is not necessarily meant to be a deliberate occupation of theirs.

There is a universal law at work. As we focus our energy on a desired target, we emit electromagnetic pulses. These waves create an energy or magnetic field, which has awesome attracting power. So when we pre-determine something, we can attract whatever is in the field of what we are determining.

While our aim may be one result, the magnetic energy draws others to us. This phenomena, is referred to as the "Law of Attraction." The Law of Attraction states that we become a magnet, attracting things to us whether desired or undesired. Our goal is to become more focused in our approach and attract only the best and what we desire to us. The other aspect of the Law of Attraction is related to the universal law of gravity. An object in motion that attracts another object is also attracted by that particular object of attraction. In other words, there is mutual attraction.

As we focus our energy toward what we desire, ultimately the object of our desire will also attract us to it. I like to refer to this as "Cooperative Energy."

Cooperative Energy is energy in motion, and working together for a common purpose. Cooperative Energy always thrives. This is why it's important to reach a higher level of awareness and consciousness. It is also of great consequence to learn how to use cooperative energy to your advantage.

Keeping your eyes on the prize, is taking hold of a vision and making it come alive. At the end of the day declare the victory. Claim your reward, whatever that may be for you.

Chapter Five Monologue: Do You Trust Me?

How blessed I am. You have come into my life during a time that I needed it most. Yes, I cry out to you in the middle of this storm of my life, and you respond to my call. You quietly listen, being considerate and careful in your responses, as your gentle voice, subdues me. I close my eyes, and I cannot imagine another who could ever make me feel as secure and as endearing as you do at this moment. Who art thou to me?

My soul is enthralled in this raging battle. For I too am feeling something internally that I have never felt before. You open me up in a way where I have dared to expose my innermost thoughts and feelings to you. I shall not fear my words haunting me. You have accepted me and loved me in spite of myself. You have grown to respect me, treating me with deferential regard and esteem. As I listen to the softness of your voice, I am captivated and delighted. I yearn to become one with you, desiring you on every level. Yet, while I am a godly man, my thoughts I'm afraid may be betraying my mind. I shall not corrupt you! My heart is to bring you to my bosom, protect you and provide for you and rescue you from the midst of this dust.

My dearest soul, you make me feel like there are no other women in this world. My eyes are fixed only on you. God has truly adorned me with His favor and sent me His Spirit in the form of a well-made man. You fill me with your grace. You take my breath away!

I adore you, my love. You satisfy every hunger in my soul. Please promise me this is real. Please tell me your words are true. Comfort me right now, darling woman. Bring my mind at ease.

I am afraid I am troubled still. I am not an unrighteous woman, but others will view me as such. How can I put your mind at ease when I am in such a humbled state and lowly condition? The Spirit has come upon me and the power of the Most High God has overshadowed me. There is a great tragedy, my love, and now all shall know the truth. That which is hidden shall come to light. What will become of me? What will become of us?

What are you saying to me? I would never want to disgrace you. Shall I privately and quietly fade away? Others will slander and gossip and say we have gone beyond all boundaries. Tell me now what is on your mind. What are you saying to me, my sweetness? This seems like such an impossible deed.

Oh my love! My heart was heavy. My mind was cloudy. I thought it was a dream. I thought maybe it was wishful thinking. Can this be from God, oh dearest and God-fearing man? Don't leave me now!

Please don't leave me now! God will never forsake us. He sent an angel. He sent His spirit. Stand in the presence of the Lord, my love! You are the strong man of God. You are God's able-bodied one. God is your might. God is your strength. Believe me! I trust you.

This will be an arduous journey. To bring such a thing forth won't be easy. Yet God has spoken to me from the depths of my soul. As I measure and weigh this in my mind, reflecting God's wisdom and only tender consideration for you my love, I take you as my wife. I commit wholly and entirely to you, my dearest love. Together we shall be victorious!

I believe you. Shield and protect me. Please, secure me and keep me safe with God's help. You are a righteous man and I am a righteous woman. What comes forth from us is blessed indeed. The visitor in the night told me so. We must trust, we must believe.

God shall increase me. He shall hold me up and expand my breast to remain faithful and dutiful to you, my wife. We shall bring the light forth together. This light shall be the truth and a living testament of our love. Fear not!

My name shall be remembered. I shall not claim to be a sea of bitterness spreading wide and far; nor shall I drink from the cup of bitter water. A complex creature indeed, but I am agreeable. At times, it may appear that I may be hard to bear with, my beloved husband, yet know and be assured that God has placed me here as a helping friend and companion to you. I shall in my nature not only comfort and nurture you, but I shall also be that vessel God uses to separate everything from you that is not worthy of your cause.

Our love shall be a sonnet spoken of for years to come. The manner in which we love and work together shall be remembered and we shall continue to inspire and uplift even from the grave. Our children shall be blessed. Our friends shall be blessed. Doors far and near shall be opened up to us and our offspring. We shall thrive in all endeavors, for my dearest husband, we surely art blessed!

The journey we embark upon shall be one we take together, my loveliest. Our love shall grant us a fortune to extend to all generations. This journey is magical and the process we dare to enjoy. Every step, every mile, let us experience all earthly pleasures. When it is done, let us be gracious to accept the divine and wonderful rewards for walking the good walk and fighting the good fight. The love we share, let us, my dear wife, let us transfer that into this beautiful butterfly yet to behold the world.

Life's Lesson:

As we embark upon the process to become what we are destined to become, and as we engage in doing what we are purposed to do, we may encounter forces that work in contrary to that great achievement. Yet, the key to forging through those obstacles is a concerted effort from within. It has been said that anything worth having or obtaining does not come easy, so expect difficulty to be attached to it. However, let not that difficulty discourage you from what it is you want to accomplish. You can achieve it! Accept nothing less.

When looking at the process of conception, one can observe millions of sperm competing to be the first

Keeping Your Eyes on the Prize

to reach and fertilize the ovum. A mature egg breaks free from the ovary and travels through the fallopian tubes and makes itself available for fertilization. Although millions of sperm start the race, most fall out of the contest fairly quickly. After that, about a hundred continue the journey. However, only one proves to be the survivor of the fittest.

The one sperm that actually reaches the egg, qualifies itself by competing. It is made fit during the process. Every journey in life operates on the same principle as that of sperm and ovum. While struggle may be attached to anything of value, we can prevail over and conquer those stumbling blocks that cause us to struggle in order to reach our destination. As the saying goes, "the race is not to the swift, nor the strong, but to those who can endure until the end." The end is the end of the struggle you may have to go through to reach your goal.

Words of Wisdom:

❖ The integrity of your intentions, determines the character of your creation.

❖ Your willingness and the course of action you take to modify counterproductive behaviors which hinder you from accomplishing your goal, is the exercise that gets you into shape and enables you to reach your goal.

❖ A prepared and committed mind is a mind that has been made up. To be double-minded is to be undecided.

❖ A healthy marriage is when two people say, "I will," then do.

❖ No one has ever won a race, they haven't run; nor completed a task they haven't begun.

WORKBOOK PART 5

Section I – Your Life Mission Statement

Directions for Writing Your Life Mission Statement: Write a mission statement for your life. This mission should encompass what you love to do and was born to do. It is a brief statement, about 3 – 4 sentences at the most.

This is YOUR PERSONAL Mission statement, and not predicated on someone else's mission for your life. You will most likely revise it several times before constructing a final mission statement. Also, during the course of your life, you may find that you will refine it several times. Remember to revisit your life mission statement often and examine it at least once per year to see if it is in need of revision.

Points to Consider as You Structure Your Life Mission Statement:

❖ Create a list of what you want to do in life.

❖ Write down three to four things that you would do even if you did not get paid to do it.

- ❖ Write down the one thing that no matter what else you do, you seem to go back to it over and over again.

- ❖ Now, the above thing is most likely what you have been born to do. So if you choose, draft your mission around that one thing.

Observations & Thoughts
Journal your observations and thoughts here from Part 5, Section I

Section II – Setting Primary Goals

Directions for Setting Primary Goals: It's important to establish primary goals so that you have something tangible to work toward. Goal lists help you to keep your eyes on the prize and offer constant reminders so that you are able to stay focused.

It is good to outline no more than four (4) goals at a time. Post these goals in all regularly visited areas such as: On the refrigerator, bathroom mirror, bedroom mirror, etc. Remember to put time frames on goal achievements. (e.g. I will lose 20-lbs by *include date*).

Guide to Setting Primary Goals:

1) The goal must inspire you.

2) The goal must be separate than another primary goal.

3) The goal should be very challenging and achievable.

4) The goal must be stated in one sentence.

5) The goal must be measurable.

GOAL 1:

GOAL 2:

GOAL 3:

GOAL 4:

Observations & Thoughts
Journal your observations and thoughts here from Part 5, Section II

Section III – Creating a Vision

Directions for Creating a Vision: Whenever you are working to accomplish something in your life, it's very important to be able to visualize what it looks like. Creating a Vision is an exercise that helps you to create the vision and keep it at the forefront of your daily life.

CREATE A VISION BOARD:

- ❖ Be creative
- ❖ Make it look very appealing
- ❖ Include various areas of your life
- ❖ Include the vision of your goal achievement

- ❖ Use photos, words, magazine photos and more
- ❖ Make it very colorful and lively
- ❖ Keep your Vision Board in an area where you can see it everyday
- ❖ Make it as large as you want

CREATE POCKET CUES OR REMINDERS:

- ❖ Use pocket notes to remind you of your goals
- ❖ Carry trinkets that remind you of what you need to do
- ❖ Carry a reminder of why you are doing what you are doing
- ❖ Keep in your pocket encouragements to help you stay focused

OUTLINE YOUR GOALS AS PROMISES TO YOURSELF & ANSWER THE FOLLOWING QUESTIONS:

- ❖ WHAT you want to accomplish?
- ❖ WHEN you want to accomplish it?
- ❖ WHERE you will do the work to accomplish it?
- ❖ WHY do you want to accomplish it?
- ❖ WHO will benefit and WHO you need to accomplish it?
- ❖ HOW will you accomplish it? (List the steps)

Observations & Thoughts
Journal your observations and thoughts here from
Part 5, Section III

Conclusion

Through ordinary people happens extraordinary things. This journey is about Y-O-U discovering your extraordinary self and the extraordinary things that you are able to do. Although there may be challenges along the way, each of us has the power to overcome them.

Book One is about preparing and committing to a life-long process of transformation. It's about making yourself ready to become a new person and staying constantly renewed at every point and time in your life. Further, it is about standing firmly on the principles of truth and being true to who you are. This first book in a series of three helps you to fix your mind on the journey and assists you in developing a new mindset to complete the journey.

In the first chapter, Knowing and Embracing Who You Are, we discussed the importance of drawing from the many experiences in life and getting acquainted with how those experiences impacted you and how they were deliberately placed there to get you to the point where you are now. In addition, the first chapter encouraged you to accept yourself as you are and to receive yourself and your experiences openly and gladly without guilt, shame or fear of judgment.

This step of the journey takes you to the place where you may just be yourself, and open completely up to trust yourself. It allows you to draw yourself in and offer yourself the loving-kindness needed to begin a transformation process. It is about you learning to love and embrace yourself without condition.

The second chapter, Assessing and Being Who You Are, forces you to look within lovingly to estimate your own self-worth and value, so that you may form a more accurate view of yourself. It allows you to judge yourself and your character truthfully and correctly. This chapter gives you evidence about yourself to examine and weigh. It helps you to verify that you do belong and have always been a consideration, made complete, lacking no essential character or essence. It gives you an amazing glimpse of the Creator and inspires you to look within yourself, who is conceived of THE ONE.

The third chapter, Learning to Love the You that You Discover, arouses you to modify your behavior through consistent practices that demonstrate a healthy view and acceptance of yourself and your purpose. It is a launching pad to your unfolding. It's about discovering the beautiful being that you are.

The fourth chapter, Exercising Your Power to Be, thrusts you into a battle of wills and competing forces. This requires you to actively engage in physical and mental exertion to bring your best self to the forefront. The battles of wills are contradictions of your own thoughts. The process to achieve internal harmony commands you to bring yourself wholly and committed to the contest. This internal conflict compels you to work hard and subjects you to put into practice what is in your nature to do in order to maintain your peace and contentment of mind.

The fifth chapter, Keeping Your Eyes on the Prize, helps you to maintain the intention of your mind and your purpose. Your true purpose is written across your heart. This chapter convinces you that the journey takes heart and before ever stepping up to the plate, you must have a heart that is ready and committed to this race!

The journey is awesome and can be oh so beautiful! Sometimes the terrain can be tumultuous; but will you quit during those turbulent times? This is a personal journey with a road that is shared. Forge your way, not at the expense of others, but by a higher inspiration. Treat others how you choose to be treated, staying humble and never giving up. Remember to handle yourself in the same manner that you desire others to handle you.

You will meet a lot of people along the way. The authentic you will manifest like an onion with many layers. You will continue to evolve over time. Your transformation will be gradual, yet you will be transformed.

To some, it may appear that a new you flourishes at every turn. Step-by-step and phase-by-phase change seems to happen. Yet, through it all, you will become who you are destined to be! There is absolutely no doubt about it!

Conclusion

As you take flight, do not be ashamed to soar far above that which keeps you away from your destiny. The journey from ordinary to extraordinary is a phenomenal experience. It's a glorious and precious gift. It's a trip of a lifetime! You deserve it, and you deserve to feel the magic in the process. So, seize this moment, and every moment hereafter, and know that success is yours!

Step out on that platform not just believing, but knowing that you are already the extraordinary person that you have set out to become. So, why not accept the truth of who you are. Why not accept and be who you are?

This is just the beginning. Will you stop now or will you continue the process? Please, continue to walk with me. Continue to be a traveling companion on this wonderful expedition. Now that you have prepared and made a total commitment, let's continue. We have not reached our destination yet. We are somewhere between ordinary and extraordinary. Look for Book Two of From Ordinary to Extraordinary: Walking in Your Purpose.

There is much work yet to do!

~The End of This Leg of the Journey~
Continue Traveling With me With Book Two

About the Author

Atiya, founder of The Marriage Tree, has over the past 20 years, dedicated her life to honing her craft and, indeed, her calling – to empower, build and maximize human potential by affecting profound transformation in people's attitudes, perspectives and behaviors. She has been the catalyst responsible for inspiring countless people worldwide to realize their dreams and achieve joy, success and fulfillment in life.

Now she's bringing all her past experiences, education, and business-development skills from her considerable history as a speaker, author and life coach to focus on her core message: marital harmony ~ extended and profound.

Yes! It is possible to have an enduring relationship that is a positive and rewarding experience for both partners. But like anything of value, it requires fine-tuning and the willingness to learn to navigate the intricacies and subtleties of the changes any marriage encounters during its lifetime. Marriage is organic – it changes, evolves, grows - or like many living things, without proper nurturing, it can deteriorate. But the good news is: it doesn't have to break down. Building a history is a worthwhile, satisfying goal, as well as a tangible legacy for your children.

Atiya is at once an optimist and a pragmatist. She's a firm believer in the reality of a happy and satisfying long term marriage. But she's no PollyAnna, having herself encountered the vagaries of marriages over the past 21 years. She has come through them stronger and happier, gratefully committed, and she can help you to achieve the same result! She'll be the first to tell that what she's going to show you won't be easy, but she's sure of one thing – it will be worth it!

You deserve to live a life filled with mutual inspiration and genuine respect. Atiya has the resources – intellectually and empathetically - to guide you to fruitful solutions that will not only positively-impact your relationship, but, as importantly, will leave you personally empowered.

Also by Atiya

Purposeful Dating

Hidden Pearls

Petals of a Rose

The Beauty of Being Free

Love is Not a Game

Overcoming the Pain of Losing a Mother

OVERALL COMMENTS ABOUT THE JOURNEY THUS FAR:

(Write your thoughts here)

www.ingramcontent.com/pod-product-compliance
Lightning Source LLC
Chambersburg PA
CBHW060530100426
42743CB00009B/1479